ARCHAEOLOGY
IN ROMANIA

ARCHAEOLOGY IN ROMANIA
The Mystery of the Roman Occupation

by

Andrew MacKenzie

Andrew MacKenzie 1986
First published in Great Britain 1986

ISBN 0 7090 2724 9

Robert Hale Limited
Clerkenwell House
Clerkenwell Green
London, EC1R 0HT

Printed and bound in Great Britain
by Unified Printers and Publishers
Ltd., 170 Brick Lane, London E1

Contents

Acknowledgements

I wish to thank Professor Constantin Preda, Director of the Institute of Archaeology, Bucharest, for his help and encouragement in research for this book, Dr Adrian V. Rădulescu, Director of the Museum of History and Archaeology at Constanţa, Dr. Florea Costea, Deputy Director and Chief Archaeologist at the Museum of History and Archaeology in Braşov, Dr Iuliu Paul, Professor of Archaeology at Sibiu University, Professor Claudia Cerchez, who is in charge of the archaeological section of the Brukenthal Museum, Sibiu, and Dr Florin Constantiniu, of the Institute of History, Bucharest, for help and advice. I wish also to thank the Cambridge University Press for permission to quote from R.W. Seton-Watson's *History of the Roumanians*.

Chronology

BC 1,000,000	Beginning of process of birth of mankind in the Carpathians-Danube area. Paleolithic.
BC 2500-2000	Influx of semi-nomadic horsemen from Western Asia form an old Eastern and Central European Population. The process of Europeanization.
BC 2000	Bronze metallurgy introduced on Romanian soil. Thracian communities of the Bronze Age flourish.
BC 1400	Aegean migration begins.
BC 1200	Birth of Early Halstatt "Iron Age" culture. Geto-Dacian peoples formed.
BC 657	Greek colonists arrive in Histria. Greeks probably arrive in Tomis (now Constanţa) early in sixth century and in Callatis (now Mangalia) at close of sixth century.
BC 514	Sixth-century arrival of the Scythians. Getae mentioned in historical records for first time by Herodotus. Fourth century. Celts settle in north-west Dacia. Third century. Dacians living in the mountains build up a tribal relationship.
BC 70-44	Burebista unites the Geto-Dacian tribes in campaign of conquests and lays foundation of Geto-Dacian state.
BC 29-28	Romans crush the local populations. Dobrudja incorporated into sphere of Roman authority.
AD 85	Dacians defeat Romans at the start of a series of wars in which honours were even until Trajan became Emperor.
AD 87	Decebalus became King of Dacia.

AD 101–102	Trajan's army defeated in mountains by King Decebalus of the Dacians but his allies are decisively defeated at Adamclisi in Dobrudja.
AD 105–106	Trajan defeats Decebalus in the Orăştie Mountains. Dacia becomes a Roman province.
AD 274–275	Emperor Aurelian withdraws army and administration from Dacia but settlers of Dacian and Roman stock remain on abandoned territory and this leads to the Dacian-Roman symbiosis and the formation of the Romanian people in the seventh to ninth centuries.
AD 896	Arrival of the Magyars into the Pannonia plain and later they gradually extend their hold over Transylvania.
AD 1330	Basarab defeats Hungarians and ensures independence of Wallachia.
AD 1359	Independent Moldavian state formed.
AD 1600	Michael the Brave unites briefly the three Romanian countries of Wallachia, Moldavia and Transylvania.
AD 1859	Union of Wallachia and Moldavia under same prince Colonel A. I. Cuza, who is later deposed.
AD 1867	Transylvania incorporated within Hungary.
AD 1881	Prince Charles I of Romania becomes king.
AD 1918	Transylvania reunited with Romania.
AD 1947	King Michael abdicates. Romania becomes a People's Republic.
AD 1965	Official name of country designated as Socialist Republic of Romania.

Introduction

One of the great mysteries of European history concerns what happened to the territory now covered by modern Romania when the Emperor Aurelian withdrew his army and administration from north of the Danube to south of the river between AD 271 and 275 — historians differ about the date. In his *History of the Roumanians* (Cambridge University Press, 1934), a book now very difficult to obtain, that eminent scholar the late Professor R. W. Seton-Watson, who held the chair of Masaryk Professor of Central European History at London University, said that, "We are dealing with perhaps the most obscure corner of Western history" and that, "There is simply no parallel for the mysterious silence which surrounds the Romanians in the thousand years following the withdrawal of Aurelian and his legions, a period in which there are neither chronicles nor charters nor archaeological remains". This was, of course written over fifty years ago, and now, mainly as a result of archaeological discoveries, a great deal is known in Romania about life in the territory following Aurelian's departure, but this knowledge is contained mainly in specialist publications and is little known to the general public in the West, or to specialists for that matter.

The question of whether the original Dacians or Daco-Roman stock survived the withdrawal of the Roman legions, or were shipped south of the Danube with the soldiers and administrators, is not just one for historians. It is a matter which has determined national attitudes. On the one hand, the Romanians have argued for the continuation of the race on their own soil; on the other, the Hungarians have said that in Transylvania they came into mainly empty territory which was theirs by right of occupation and conquest. The Hungarian attitude to the problem is given in *Chambers's Encyclo-*

pedia, volume 13, by a contributor who says that "Whether Transylvania contained any Romanian population at the time of the Hungarian conquest continues to be a matter of controversy between rival national historians. Romanians are recorded in early documents, although not in the earliest, figuring only in one area, and there only for a short period, as enjoying corporate organisation on a large scale. They usually appear as masterless men or serfs, but some achieved Hungarian nobility." The author of this piece quoted Makkai's *Histoire de Transylvanie* (1946), stating that it was "written from the Hungarian angle but embodying the result of much modern research". However, this could not have included archaeological research on Romanian soil, and a totally different picture of the situation at the time of the Hungarian invasion in the ninth and tenth centuries is given in this book, which is based on the results of archaeological research. Not only have I interviewed archaeologists at the Institute of Archaeology at Bucharest and in museums and universities throughout Romania but I have also gone into the field with them to inspect sites.

In order that references to critics of the Romanian attitude may be placed in context, I will quote R. W. Seton-Watson's interpretation of the Hungarian viewpoint. He says that :

> *The Magyars... argue that the continuity [of the Romanians] is a myth ; that the abandonment of the Roman element was complete; that in any case Romanization of the province cannot really have struck very deep in so short a period as 163 years, and that of the colonists who originally crossed the Danube, the great mass was not of Roman blood at all. Arguing from the large admixture of Slav elements in the modern Romanian language, they lay greater stress upon the Slavonic than upon their Latin origin. They point to the absence of any records showing them to have occupied their present territory during the Dark Ages, and proceed to argue that the Romanians of today are descended from nomadic Balkan tribes who only crossed to the north bank of the Danube in the thirteenth century, and then gradually overflowed into Transylvania in response to the welcome extended by the Hungarian kings to foreign settlers.*

Seton-Watson is doubtful about this argument. He points out that the lack of records is due to a double cause — that throughout these south-eastern territories really ordered life can be said to begin only after the twelfth century, and that the terrible Mongol invasion which devastated Hungary in 1241 was responsible for a wholesale destruction of such records as existed. The "weakness" of the theory that the Romanians reached their present home only in the thirteenth century begins to emerge, he says, if we ask its mainly Hungarian authors to explain what on their showing became of the Romanians during the nine centuries which elapsed during their withdrawal by Aurelian and their reappearance as a budding state in the thirteenth century. It cannot be maintained that they continued to inhabit northern Moesia after it was rechristened Dacia, for we know that province to have been submerged by Slav invasions and to have re-emerged long before the period in question as one of the most purely Slavonic states in Europe. "The very theorists who have banished the Romanians from Transylvania for lack of records are driven to admit an even more complete and far more perplexing lack of records regarding the Romanians in their alleged Balkan home."

Seton-Watson also said that, without desiring to dogmatize on a subject which has been rightly described as "an enigma of the Middle Ages", he ventured to think that a much more *logical* and *simple* explanation was provided by the assumption that the modern Romanians, who fell into two main groups — the so-called Daco-Romanians and Macedo-Romanians — owed their survival to the shelter provided by high mountain ranges, inhospitable and difficult of access in early times — in the south the Pindus, in the north the Carpathians. "What more natural than that it should serve as a refuge during the long centuries of invasion, and that the survivors should issue forth into the plains when at last the tide of invasion began to subside?"

In addition to the mountains, shelter could be obtained in the thick forests both in the mountains and in the Danube plain. Paths through these forests would be known to the local inhabitants but not to invaders.

In view of Seton-Watson's remarks about the early inhabitants of Romania taking to the hills at times of invasion, I expected to be taken at least to the foothills for sites of early settlements but, to my surprise, I was escorted to river valleys, where settlements abounded. For instance, in Șercaia, a commune of six thousand people fifty-one kilometres from Brașov and fifteen from Făgăraș, archaeologists have found in one square kilometre remains of thirty-three small villages which were occupied by Daco-Roman families. In an area of eighty by eighty kilometres through which the River Olt flows, eight hundred sites from various periods have been excavated.

The opponents of the Romanian view on the continuity of their race, base their views on the writings of the German geographer Robert Roesler (1840-81), who claimed that the ancestors of the Romanians of today crossed to the north bank of the Danube only in the thirteenth century. When I discussed this point at the Institute of Archaeology, the veteran archaeologist Mrs Eugenia Zaharia told me that there was no archaeological evidence of a large influx of population at the relevant time to support this view, and the Director of the Institute, Dr. Constantin Preda, added that no evidence had been found of a fall in the population of the south bank of the Danube in the thirteenth century. Also, if such a migration had occurred, as maintained by Roesler's supporters, the population of Romania could be expected to have many more people of Slav origin than was in fact the case.

Professor Preda told me that remains of settlements dating from between the third and eleventh centuries have been found all over Romania, one third of them in Transylvania, and, with cemeteries, numbered "thousands". Since the end of the Second World War archaeological excavations in Romania had started with fortresses in the hills and only later extended to valleys. There was not enough proof of the continuity of the race before 1949. For twenty years there was a gap between the sixth and tenth centuries, but this gap had now been filled.

What was the population of Transylvania, the supposed "empty land", between the time of the departure of Aurelian and the arrival of the Hungarians? I asked Professor Iuliu Paul, who holds the chair of archaeology at Sibiu University. He answered that, based on the number of settlements found, it must have been about one million. The population of the whole of Romania, including Transylvania, was then about three million.

Archaeology has turned out to be the richest and most direct source in proving the process of Dacian continuity. Romanian archaeological researches during the last quarter of a century have produced previously unknown material traces which can be attributed without any doubt to the Dacian population from the period of the Roman domination.

On the territory of the former Roman province of Dacia (Transylvania, Banat and Oltenia), researchers have discovered many traces of the post-Aurelian culture, which provides convincing proof of the persistence of the Daco-Roman population in the countryside as well as in the urban and military centres. This proof consists of settlements that have been excavated, fortresses, documents, inscriptions, buildings of various types, the contents of cemeteries, ceramics, tools, household goods, jewellery and, in particular, coins. An analysis of the monetary treasures found in Transylvania, as in the rest of the province, established that the process of accumulation of them started in the first century AD and continued during the Roman epoch in the second and third centuries. The many owners of these treasures belonged to the Geto-Dacian society which collected coins before and after the Roman conquest. Among the monetary treasures of Transylvania are those discovered at Alba Iulia, Alecuș, Dimbău, Hunedoara, Jeledinți, Lăpușnic, Reghin, Tibodu and Vișea. In each of these places Roman imperial coins from the first to the third century have been found.

Discoveries have been particularly rich in Transylvania, where proof of the many settlements that existed there counters the claims of the Hungarians that they came to what was almost an empty land. Seton-Watson says in his History that

> If the Magyar theory be accepted (and, incidentally, if the earliest Magyar chronicler, the "Anonymous Notary of King Bela" be rejected as mythical), an immense tract of country, comprising most of present-day Romania, must have been for centuries without masters — a kind of No Man's Land. Hunfalvy, probably the ablest of the controversalists, has no better explanation to offer than that Transylvania, in particular, was a neutral territory, where Magyars and Pechenegs, a Mongol tribe which survived into the 11th century, exercised

hunting rights, but where the Bulgarians [among whom, presumably, were the Romanians] were excluded. This is hardly convincing.

I will deal with this controversy later in the book, but at this stage I feel I may give my opinion that if it is admitted that Wallachia and Moldavia, which were not Hungarian lands, were populated at the time, it would be strange indeed if Transylvania, so rich in gold as to attract the Romans there at the beginning of the millennium, would be left without people. Also, if Transylvania was virtually uninhabited, as the Hungarians claim, where did the local rulers who opposed the Magyars raise their armies? We can, of course, go on asking such questions, but it is more satisfactory to indicate the number of settlements and sites of fortresses as proof that the province was inhabited and fortified when the Magyars came and leave it at that. The eminent Romanian historian Dr Ștefan Pascu said in the quarterly publication *Pages of History* in 1985 that "Investigations made of late on the basis of archaeologic and written sources led to the conclusion that the number of 8th-9th century settlements ran to over 600, scattered all through the Romanian ethnic territory."

As part of their claim to continuity of race, the Romanians have published during the past two decades thirty thousand titles on historical subjects with a view to the enrichment and improvement of documentation. Pointing this out in the article în *Pages of History* from which I just quoted, Professor Pascu, paying tribute to the works of the country's archaeologists, said that

> *Over 1,000 discoveries : settlements, necropolises, hoards, 4th-11th century coins of Daco-Roman tradition, scattered all through this country's territories, including the territories of the free Dacians, differing only in their circulation intensity (more frequent in the intra-Carpathian zone, with average circulation between the Carpathians and the Danube, slightly greater east of the Carpathians), come to prove the continuity of the Daco-Roman population and later of the Romanian people in the Carpathian-Danubian-Pontic space.*
>
> *Linguistic and historical studies attest to the completion of the ethnogenesis process in the 7th*

and 8th centuries, when a new people, the Romanian
one, was recorded on Europe's ethno-political
map...

The Romanians feel very deeply about attacks on their
racial origins by Hungarians and others. In his book *The*
"Sick Heart" of Modern Europe, (Washington, 1975) the
late Professor Hugh Seton-Watson, son of R. W. Seton-
Watson, after discussing how the Romanians defeated
Russian attempts to rewrite their history, "the ultimate
aim no doubt being to show that the Romanians were
not "Latins" but "Slavs", said that :

> *To be deprived of one's national history, to see*
> *one's national identity threatened, is something*
> *which Americans or West Europeans can hardly*
> *imagine happening to them. Historians should not,*
> *of course, overrate their own importance, but from*
> *some experience I am fairly sure of one thing: in*
> *the Danube countries, national history, or if you*
> *like historical mythology, is something about which*
> *not only professors of history but also working men*
> *and women, in factories and farms, feel bitterly.*
> *Attacks on it create a smouldering resentment which*
> *does not die out and can easily turn into a flame.*

Because of the political realities of the Balkans
— Romania and Hungary are both Communist countries
within the Warsaw Pact — the dispute about who were
the original inhabitants of Transylvania has been contained and no claim has been put forward by Hungarians for boundary changes. However, in indirect ways,
such as by suggesting that they have a greater historical
claim to Transylvania than the Romanians and that the
substantial Hungarian-speaking minority there is being
persecuted, the Hungarians have contrived to conduct a
campaign in which the belief is fostered that Transylvania is really a Hungarian land wrongly occupied
by the Romanians. No matter what denials are made by
the Hungarians in Romania that they are not being ill
treated, that their children are being educated in their
own language, that the Hungarian language is used in
Church services and that they have books, magazines and
broadcasts in Hungarian, the charges of ill treatment are
repeated over and over again by *émigrés,* thus keeping
"the pot on the boil". In these circumstances the Roma-

nians have realized that the best way they can present their claim to continuity is through the evidence produced by archaeological research.

Archaeology is, therefore, strongly supported by the Romanian government, which places particular stress on the continuity of the race from the time of the Dacians, the Daco-Roman wars, the withdrawal of the Emperor Aurelian's legions, and the gradual merging of the two races, plus some strains introduced by migrants, to form the Romanian people. There is no real argument about the continuation of the race south of the Danube, but there is a very real argument, started in comparatively modern times for political purposes, about who were the first settlers in Transylvania.

Archaeology in Romania dates from 1834, when the National Museum for Antiquities was founded in Bucharest. In 1956 this museum became the Romanian Institute of Archaeology. There is another Institute for Archaeology and History at Cluj-Napoca, the ancient capital of Transylvania, and also one at Jassy (Iaşi), former capital of Moldavia. There are branches of these institutes at Craiova in Oltenia, Sibiu, Timişoara and other important towns. Indeed, nearly all towns of any size have a museum of history and archaeology, which, sadly, is not the case in centres with a similar population in the United Kingdom. In all, about three hundred archaeologists, two-thirds of them on the staff of museums, are engaged in research.

In 1985, the year of my most recent visit to Romania, about four hundred sites were being worked. Every year about twenty new ones are opened when there is clear evidence that they are important. The decision on the work to be done is made by a joint commission of the Romanian Academy and the Council for Socialist Culture and Education. Before a new building is constructed, archaeologists are allowed access to the site, and this accounts for about half the number of excavations in a year. In March archaeologists present a preliminary report on suggested sites, a budget for the work is fixed by the Government the following month, and after that the joint commission makes the selection of sites for excavation between July and September, although, if the weather is favourable, work may be extended until October. Determining factors here are the needs of agriculture and the availability of student labour. On any site students make up the bulk of the labour

force, which is always supervised by an archaeologist,
with some local inhabitants helping. Pay is at the rate of
75 lei a day, between £4 and £5 at the official rate
of exchange. Compensation is paid to farmers for the
use of their land, which is always restored to its
former state at the end of the season, although the
site may have to be opened up again in the following year.

The finding of objects during farming has led to
sites being excavated. Aerial photography, Professor
Preda said, has provided a most useful aid to archaeology, particularly in respect to fortresses, in bringing
to light features which cannot be examined easily on
the ground. Aerial photography has been used particularly in Dobrudja and Bihor.

I asked Professor Preda about the significance of
human remains when finds are being dated. Between
the second and third centuries, he said, people were
mostly cremated, as evidenced by vases found with ashes,
but after the fourth century AD, with the rise of Christianity, mourners started to bury bodies. Researchers
have recently discovered at Alba Iulia a cemetery with
more than one thousand tombs from the Roman period
until the tenth century, and in Wallachia near the Danube
(Izvorul) a cemetery with eight hundred tombs from the
eighth to the tenth century AD, and the remains of more
than three hundred bodies.

The environment in Romania has been protected by
means of legislation. In Constanţa a proposed building
was shifted to a new site so that a mosaic could be
preserved ; in Jassy work on a block of flats was halted
when remains of an old palace were uncovered : not only
was work stopped but the ruins were restored. Near
Cozia Monastery, which was built by a ruling prince of
Wallachia, Mircea the Old, in the fourteenth century, a
river was diverted so that a Roman castle would not be
disturbed.

Ceramics are particularly significant as indicators of
certain cultures at the time they were produced. The
Nobel Prize winning novelist William Golding, who is
keenly interested in Egyptology, reviewing a book on
the life of the archaeologist Flinders Petrie in *The Ob-
server* of 25 August 1985, said that:

> *Petrie realised long before the collectors, the vir-*
> *tuosos and antiquaries of the nineteenth century*

that digging was not about finding valuable objects *but about the retrieval of information, and that no scrap of pot or papyrus is without importance. A brilliant intuition told him that the shape of pots changed not in a bound but little by little and that therefore pots put together from those scraps and arranged like-by-like would give him the succession of historical events. A great deal of the Egyptian history which we accept as the general knowledge proper to an educated man comes out of those rows of pots.*

The significance of ceramics unearthed in settlements as clues to a particular people at a certain time will be considered in this book.

Archaeology, of course, involves more than excavations. One of the most important and fascinating tasks of Romania's archaeologists is the identification of the fortresses and major settlements (*davae*) named by ancient writers, particularly Ptolemy, but since lost to sight. As the aim of this book is to indicate the light archaeology throws on Dacians and Romans, the first three chapters are devoted to a general survey of the historical background, although there is much material about archaeology, and by then the ground has been prepared so that readers can be presented with more specific information about archaeological finds. Chapter Four, for instance, contains a number of accounts of how *davae* mentioned by Ptolemy have been identified.

The excavation of fortresses and settlements has thrown light on the formation of Dacian society and how it was organized. A first striking thing was the deep social division of labour. Evidence of how people lived is provided by the handicraft shops identified in the Dacian strongholds in the Orăștie Mountains, by a jeweller's shop found at Pecica, by the special tools for various crafts and trades unearthed at Bîtca Doamnei in Moldavia, and by the new kinds of pottery developed, the painted pottery, alongside the imitations of pots with Greek and Roman patterns, which imply a good command of sophisticated pottery-making techniques. These few examples taken at random prove that, together with the more traditional major branches — cattle-raising and agriculture — plus handicrafts that were supposed to meet the current needs of the common people and the ever more refined tastes of the aristocracy, they ac-

counted for a considerable share of the economy as a
whole. Unfortunately, the data available on the stage
reached by agriculture and cattle-raising — breeding
techniques, ownership etc — are far from satisfactory.
However, important archaeological evidence, such as the
carbonized seeds discovered at Grădiştea Muncelului,
Meleia and Cetăţeni, has allowed specialists to identify
some crops, such as wheat, rye, barley, lentil and hemp.
We may realize indirectly the progress made in agricultural techniques from the tools found in settlements
but we lack both pollen-analysis data, which could have
contributed more specific information on the types of
crops, and enough aerial photographs to show the possible distribution of the arable land by individual plots.
Much more work remains to be done in this field.

Romania is an ancient country: it is one of the
cradles of mankind in Europe. The late historian, archaeologist and ethnographer Dr Constantin Nicolăescu-Plopşor
led a team which in 1962 discovered a settlement where
pre-paleolithic man lived about two million years
ago. This was in Wallachia in a place known as Valea
lui Grăunceanu in Bugiuleşti commune, Vilcea county, a
spot in a gulf which at one time extended between the
present courses of the Olt, leaving a deposit between
1.8 and two million years old. In an area extending just
over 80 square metres researchers found remains of
twenty-eight species of animals, which included fossil
bears, rhinoceroses, horses, rams and apes. Since it was
out of the question that all these animals could have
lived together in such a short space, the conclusion was
drawn that this was a place where the humanoids used
to gather and feed on the animals they had killed. This
conclusion was supported by the identification of a wide
range of instruments for permanent use made of bones
of mammals, shiny through extensive use. Several
unchipped stones (which, however, showed traces of
smashing) were also found at Bugiuleşti. When it was
discovered that they did not belong to the local geolo-
gical stratum, the area of search was widened and it
was found that they had been brought from a place
known as Magura Slatinei forty-two kilometres away.
The stones were used for making bone artefacts. It followed that a deliberate activity, involving the carriage
of stones over a considerable distance for a selected
purpose implied thinking, human behaviour. Further
search brought to light three fragments of tibial and

femural disphyses which had belonged to the primate of Bugiuleşti. At that time these fragments were the only ones of their kind in the world, but eventually similar fossils were unearthed in South Africa, where their age was estimated at about two million years, and a comparison between them led to the conclusion that they belonged to the same species, *Australo-pithecus.*

In Chapter Five details are given of finds dating back nineteen thousand years in a settlement in the north of Moldavia.

It may be asked what is meant by the "original population" of Romania, the country being as old as it is. In specialist literature one comes across such terms as the "autochthonous population" but "autochthonous" as an adjective should apply to fauna and flora rather than to people of a primitive stock, who are more correctly referred to as "autochthons" "Original population" is a simpler term, and as this is a book mainly about Dacians and Romans, I have used it to describe Dacians and the Daco-Romans who inhabited the country after the withdrawal of Aurelian's legions from north of the Danube.

In short, in order to prove the continuity of the Dacians, there is a direct, rich and varied documentation that cannot be doubted, namely inscriptions, archaeological discoveries and linguistic sources which can prove that, no matter how large was the number of colonists brought to Dacia, it was lower than that of the local population, which continued to represent the main ethnic element.

In some of the chapters that follow I have drawn heavily on articles written by archaeologists and historians in *Pages of History,* with additional information supplied during interviews and on-site observations.

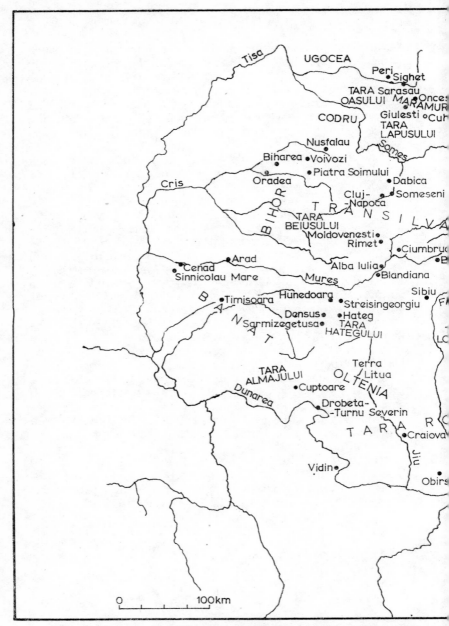

A map of Romania with sites of settlements between the eighth and fourteenth centuries. By courtesy of Dr. Radu Popa of the Institute of Archaeology, Bucharest.

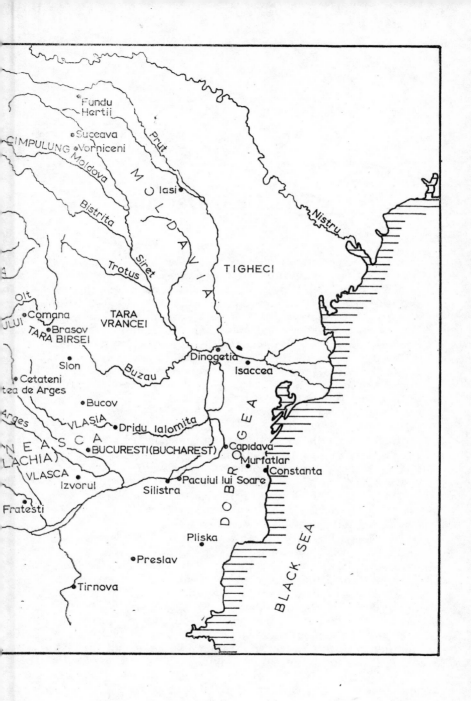

1. The Geto-Dacians

Before we set out on our archaeological trail, we should consider the background of the Geto-Dacians, ancestors of the Romanians. The population of Thracian origin from the Carpathian-Danubian and Pontic areas to the Balkans, which asserted itself in the economic and political life of south-eastern Europe until the Roman conquest, is well known in the written testimonies from ancient times under the names of Getae and Dacians. Separated from the great mass of Thracians during the seventh and sixth centuries BC, the Geto-Dacians possessed an ethnic and linguistic unity. The name "Getae" was used by Greek writers to describe all the Geto-Dacians, especially the population from the Lower Danube living on both sides of the Danube, from the Carpathians to the Black Sea and to the Balkans. Their contacts with the Greek world made possible the recording of the first news about the Getae from the sixth century BC in the works of the Greek writer Herodotus.

The name "Dacians" was preferred by Latin writers for the inhabitants of the central and western regions of the Carpathian-Danubian area, especially Transylvania, being extended later also to the population inhabiting the extra-Carpathian area, which incorporates all the Geto-Dacians. The Dacians are mentioned for the first time in written testimonies from the middle of the first century BC in Caesar's *De Bello Gallico*.

The Greek-Latin literary tradition from ancient times presents the Getae and Dacians as the same population, members of the northern branch of the great Thracian nation, speaking the same language. The ethnic identity of the Geto-Dacians and their community of language and territory are confirmed by the results of archaeological research.

The Geto-Dacians lived in a very large territory, stretching from the Balkans to the northern Carpathians and from the Black Sea and the River Tyras to the Tisa plain, sometimes even to the Middle Danube. These utmost limits of the spreading area of the Geto-Dacians correspond especially to the epoch of Burebista, of whom more later. They are confirmed by archaeological discoveries and by the map of Dacia drawn up on the basis of Agrippa's commentaries in 12 BC. The territories inhabited by the Geto-Dacians, the rivers, the towns, and the names of the Dacian tribes are mentioned in several sources. Hecateu, the Greek historian and geographer (540-470 BC) and Herodotus (sixth and seventh centuries BC), mention the Terizi and Crobizi in the south of Dobrudja, the Agatîrsi (probably Scythians assimilated by the Thracians), in Transylvania along the River Mureş, and the Sigini in the Tisa area.

According to Ptolemy's *Guide to Geography* (100-170), Dacia was inhabited by the following peoples : Piefigii, Siensii, Potulatensii (Wallachia) ; Buridavensii, Biefii, Keiagisii, Cotensii (Oltenia) ; Costobocii, Karpii, Tagrii, Piengeţii, Sabocii and Tyragetii (eastern part of the Carpathians) ; Ratacensii, Predavensii, Albocensii and Saldensii (Transylvania and Banat).

In sources from ancient times, especially in Ptolemy's *Geography,* the names of over forty locations in Dacia are mentioned, some of them being localized and identified on the basis of ancient itineraries and by archaeological research and inscriptions. Among the most important and well known are : Sarmizegetusa Regia (Grădiştea Muncelului), Napoca (Cluj), Apulum (Alba Iulia), Porolissum (Moigrad), Potaissa (Turda), Cumidava (Rîşnov), Zizidava (Pecica-Arad), Tibiscum (Jupa), Dierna (Orşova), all of them in Transylvania and Banat ; Drobeta (Turnu-Severin), Sucidava (Celei) in Oltenia ; Piroboridava (Poiana), Tamasidava (Răcătău), Zargidava (Brad), Petrodava (Piatra-Neamţ) in Moldavia ; Troesmis, Dinogeţia, Axiopolis, Sacidava, Capidava and Arcidava in Dobrudja.

Very important also is the information from ancient sources relating to the rivers of Dacia. Herodotus mentions the Danube (Istros), Porata-Pyretus (Prutul), Tiarantos (Siretul), Araros (Buzaul), Naparis (Ialomiţa), Ordessos (Argeşul) and Maris (Mureşul). Later on, other writers, particularly Ptolemy, give us information about the rivers Aluta (Olt), Tibiscum (Timiş), Samus (Someş),

Cristia (Criş) and Dierna (Cerna). Most of these names were taken over by the Romans from the Geto-Dacians, especially from those inhabiting the province of Dacia, and have been preserved by Romanians until now.

The Geto-Dacians spoke the northern dialect of the Thracian language. The only texts in Thracian are represented by two inscriptions with Greek letters preserved on a ring discovered at Ezerove and on a funeral plaque at Kiolmen, both in Bulgaria. None of these inscriptions has been deciphered. The evidence of the Thracian characteristics of the Geto-Dacian language was preserved in Strabo's works (first century BC) and especially in the works of the great Roman poet Ovid, who during his exile in Tomis (Constanţa), learned to speak and write poetry in the Getic language. The book written by Ovid in this language disappeared after his death in AD 17.

Among the words of Thraco-Dacian origin preserved until now, out of which about 170 terms have been identified, in the Romanian language, the most important seem to be the fifty-seven names of medicinal herbs recorded by Dioscurides in Greek and Latin writing. We may add to this the proper names, names of people and places, known from ancient authors and inscriptions. However, there are many terms in the Romanian language whose meaning has not yet been explained and which could proceed from the old language of the Dacians.

The Thraco-Dacian language belonged to an Indo-European group of the so-called *satem* type, being related to the Baltic, Slav, Iranian and Sanskrit languages and especially to Illyrian. This was gradually replaced by Latin, disappearing as a language during the fifth to seventh centuries. In the transition period many Thraco-Dacian words have been preserved, a part of them being taken over and used jointly by Daco-Romans and transmitted to the Romanian language.

As a result of the Geto-Dacian contacts with the Greek and Roman worlds and civilization, some isolated written elements penetrated into Dacia before the Roman conquest. Evidence is offered by some ceramic fragments discovered in the Geto-Dacian settlement in Octina (Vrancea district), carrying inscriptions with the name of the local king Thiamarcos and Latin groups of letters (BVR, REB). In the capital of Dacia before the Roman conquest, Sarmizegetusa Regia (Transylvania), researchers have found stone blocks from the defence wall with Greek capital letters printed on them. Among the ruins they also discovered a clay vessel with the inscription "DECEBALUS PER SCORILO" ("Decebalus, son of Scorilo"), representing probably the mark of a local workshop.

The religion of the Geto-Dacians attracted the attention of some writers from ancient times, as well as that of modern historians and commentators, mainly because of their faith in immortality. Herodotus tells us that the Getae "believe that they do not die but those who disappear from the world go to the God Zamolxis, who is also called Gebeleizis". The belief in immortality in the Getae's faith can also be found by references in the works of writers from ancient times such as Hellanicos (fifth century BC), Pomponius, Mela (first century AD) and Julian (fourth century AD), with explanations for the carrying out of some special rituals.

The supreme god adored by the Geto-Dacians was Zamolxis. Greek literary tradition presents him as a mortal who travelled widely and had contacts with Pythagoras (582-507 BC). According to the indications we have, Zamolxis would have been an earthy divinity, god of fertility and vegetation, gaining gradually also the symbol of Uranus and of the sun. To the memory of the great Geto-Dacian god, the people built the religious monuments of Sarmizegetusa Regia, principally the well-known Kogaionon (the Holly Mountain) about which the Greek geographer Strabo wrote in the first century BC.

In addition to the supreme divinity, the Geto-Dacians also honoured Mars, the god of war. In this respect, some records have been preserved in the works of Jordanes *(Getica)* and Ovid *(Tristele)*. The goddess Artemis was known to the Thracians under the name of Bendis, goddess of the moon, forests and spells. Among the divinities of the Thracians and also of the Geto-Dacians, there was a god of the sun, protector of vegetation, healer and wizard, whose cult is attested from the Bronze Age by votive chariots carried by birds (Bujorul, Teleorman district and Orăştie, Hunedoara district, both in Transylvania). One can add to this the cult of the Thracian Knight, a divinity of wild nature and of spring, and that of the Danubian Knight, both divinities of Geto-Dacian origin from the second to fourth centuries AD. I have examined many plaques portraying these divinities in Romanian museums. a feature of them being that the horseman is almost invariably shown as proceeding from left to right.

The first political assertion of the Geto-Dacians recorded in ancient sources dates from about the end of the sixth century BC. Writing about Darius I's expedition against the Scythians from the northern part of the Black Sea (514-513 BC), Herodotus recalls the resistance opposed to the Persian king by the Getae, mentioning that, "Before reaching the River Istru, he first defeated the Getae, who believe themselves immortal..., and because they behaved foolishly have been enslaved, although they were the bravest and most honest of the Thracians". By analysing the text and especially by examination of archaeological discoveries, one finds that the Getae who resisted the Persian armies were organized in a union of tribes situated in the northern part of Dobrudja, led most probably by a king. In one of his tragedies (*Piloctetes,* fifth century BC), Sophocles mentions the name of King Chalcodon, who ruled over the Getae, a proof that from the sixth to fifth centuries BC the Getae had reached the level of being organized in socio-political formations, well established and structured, and were able to defend their liberty.

The attempt by the Scythians, led by Ateas, to penetrate the south of the Danube in the Dobrudja area (339 BC) met the resistance of the inhabitants of Histria, namely the Getae and their king. Called by Ateas for help, the Macedonian king Philip II went to Dobrudja, where, after the death of the King of Histria, he came into conflict with the Scythians, whom he defeated. According to Arrian, in 335 BC, during his campaign against the Triballians, Alexander the Great reached the Danube, where he was faced by a great number of Getae. The Macedonian army, consisting of fifteen hundred horsemen and four hundred infantrymen, crossed the Danube during the night, using small local boats (*monoxile*). "The Macedonians met here large and rich cornfields, where the soldiers were cutting their way through, bowing the corn with their spears." The Getae retreated to the countryside where, wisely, Alexander did not pursue them. In 326 BC, according to Justinus, a Macedonian army led by General Zopirion against the Scythians from the north Pontiac steppes, was defeated by the Getae near the Danube while returning from the campaign. Zopirion himself disappeared in the battle. Between 297 and 292 BC the north Danubian Getae, led by their king Dromichaites, were in conflict with King Lysimachus of Thrace, who had conquered some Getic towns and territories of the Danube. According to Diodor of Sicily, the Getae were twice victorious. In the first battle Agathocles, son of Lysimachus, was captured and afterwards liberated by the Getae with the hope that "by such act of generosity they would recover their lost territories". In the second battle the King of Thrace was captured. The King was taken to the Getic fortress of Helis (so far unidentified), where he was treated with hospitality by Dromichaites and then liberated. The magnanimity of the Getic king made Lysimachus give back to the Getae the conquered fortresses and express his regrets for making war against them.

From an inscription of the third century BC discovered at Histria, it follows that the Greek city asked for help from King Zalmodegikos, to whom they committed sixty hostages and the "property" of the fortress. In all probability, Zalmodegikos was the chieftain of the union of Getic tribes of the area stretching from the Lower Siret and the valley of the Buzău river. It follows from another inscription of about 200 BC that King Rhemaxos, chieftain of the same north Danubian Getic tribes, was called to save the city of Histria and its crops from the threat of King Zoltes's Thracians.

The writer Trogus Pompeius reports that the Geto-Dacian King Oroles, who ruled the east Carpathian parts of Dacia and the eastern parts of Transylvania, probably about 200 BC, punished his subjects because they lost the battle against the Bastarnians. The same source mentions that the power of the Dacians rose under the reign of King Rubobostes, who ruled intra-Carpathian Dacia (Transylvania) in the second century BC. Recent studies suggest that Rubobostes was none other than Burebista, a ruler of outstanding ability.

Written sources (Dion Chrisostomos) attest that Burebista was considered a great personality in Dacia even from 80 BC. It seems that he started the process of unification first as a chieftain of the Getae established between the Danube and the Carpathians. Gradually he managed to unify all the territories inhabited by the Geto-Dacians, establishing the capital in intra-Carpathian Dacia (Transylvania) in the mountains of Hunedoara.

The essential work achieved by Burebista was the unification of all the Geto-Dacians and the raising of

Dacia to the level of one of the most important kingdoms of the ancient world. Strabo wrote: "Coming to rule his people who were tired because of many wars, Burebista so uplifted them through drills, abstention from wine and obedience that in a few years he built a strong state [empire] and subjected to the Getae most of the neighbouring populations." In this outstanding achievement Burebista was helped by the great priest Decenau. The ancient historian Jordanes wrote that Decenau had been given "an almost royal power". The strong spiritual influence inaugurated by Decenau contributed to a large extent to the unification of the Geto-Dacians.

In all probability Burebista became the king of all the Geto-Dacians from the extra — and intra-Carpathian region by 70 BC. After that date he concentrated on the consolidation of the economic and political unity of the newly created kingdom. Strabo stated that : "The number of Geto-Dacians rose greatly so that they could send to battle over 200,000 men." In front of a strong and well-trained army in 60 BC, Burebista succeeded in defeating the Celts, the Boii and the Taurisci and extended his power to the Middle Danube, including within the bounds of his kingdom all the Dacians living west to the Tisa River.

Such a power could not leave apart the western shore of the Black Sea and the towns which economically dominated this area. Therefore, in 55 BC the Geto-Dacian king made for the Pontus Euxinus and succeeded in encompassing all the Greek cities from Olbia to Apollonia within his kingdom.

After these events Burebista became, as it appears in an inscription on stone discovered at Dionysopolis (Balcic), "the first and greatest of the kings of Thrace, master of the regions on both sides of the Danube" and, as Strabo said, "Even the Romans came to fear him."

In 48 BC Burebista and his state had reached the top of their power, Dacia becoming the greatest power in south-east Europe. Although Geto-Dacian society did not know the division of social classes, it still had a few differentiated social strata. Written sources mention the existence of a ruling class, known as *tarabostes* (*pilleati*) from among whom they elected the kings and the priests, and the free common people called *comati* (*capilati*). Through Acornion of Dionysopolis, the great Geto-Dacian king made contact with Pompey, to whom he offered military support in his fight with Julius

Caesar. After defeating Pompey, Caesar made plans for a big expedition against Burebista but he could not realize them because he was murdered in 44 BC.

About this time Burebista also disappeared from the political scene in Dacia. Strabo relates that, "He died because of a rebellion before the Romans could send an army against him." It is supposed that he died, as did his enemy Caesar, by a Court conspiracy aimed to take over his power or to share it.

Immediately after Burebista's death the state created by him was divided. Strabo said that, "His successors parted, crumbling the power", at the beginning in four parts, and in Augustus's time in five "small states". But this division did not mean the end of the Dacian state. Written sources and archaeological remains tell us that the principal nucleus of the state, with its centre in Transylvania, persisted and was consolidated gradually until the Roman conquest of Dacia. The names of several Geto-Dacian kings, mentioned by Jordanes (sixth century AD) are connected with this nucleus of the state. From that source we know that after Burebista Deceneu mounted the throne, and then power was taken over by Comosicus, as both king and priest. After Comosicus, for a period of forty years, the Dacian state was led by King Corylus, probably the "Scorylo" mentioned by the Latin writer Frontinus. This list ends with King Diurpaneus, probably the "Duras" mentioned by the Latin historian Dio Cassius, and he gave up the throne to Decebalus. All these kings led the nucleus of the main Dacian state in Transylvania, with Sarmizegetusa Regia as its capital. The history of extra-Carpathian Dacia after Burebista's death was closely connected with Rome's policy in the Balkans. The Greek writer Plutarch (first and second centuries AD) spoke about the Getian King Dicomes who offered military support in exchange for payment to Mark Antony in his fight against Augustus.

By that time Cotison was king of the south-western parts of Dacia. The writer Florus (second century AD) said that during the dispute for power in Rome between Octavian (Augustus) and Mark Antony, "The Dacians who live close to mountains under the leadership of King Cotison used to come down and devastate the neighbouring territories whenever the Danube was frozen."

During the same period, in the Getic region between the Danube and the Black Sea (Dobrudja), written sources mention three Geto-Dacian kings : Roles, Dapyx and

Zyraxes. The first was the leader in the southern part of Dobrudja ; the other two shared together the middle and northern parts of the territory. As Dio Cassius said, Roles became "ally and friend of the Romans", especially after the help he gave to Licinius Crassus in his victorious battle against the Bastarnians. In 29 BC Roles met Octavian at Corinth. Being in strife with Dapyx, his neighbour from the north, Roles asked Licinius Crassus for support. Crassus came back to Dobrudja, defeated Dapyx, who committed suicide, and went to war against Zyraxes. On that occasion the Getic fortress Genuela was conquered and the Getic king was forced to take refuge in the north of the Danube. Starting with 27 BC, when Crassus celebrated his victory in Rome, the Empire's borders were established along the Danube.

Under Burebista's reign and afterwards until the Roman conquest, Geto-Dacian culture reached the highest level of its evolution. The settlements called *davae* flourished. The most important were those of Popeşti, Cră-şani, Cetăţeni, Cîrlomăneşti, Sprîncenata (Wallachia) ; Ocniţa (Oltenia) ; Pecica (Banat) ; Cugir, Piatra Craivii, Sîncrăieni (Transylvania) ; Cîndeşti, Poiana, Brad and Răcătău (Moldavia). In the same period fortresses were built in Dacia with stone walls cut after the Greek techniques. Such fortresses were raised in Transylvania on high hills, even mountains, at what is now Grădiştea Muncelului, where the capital of the Geto-Dacians, Sarmizegetusa Regia, was built, at Coteşti, Blidaru and Piatra Roşie, all in the area of the Orăştie Mountains, at Băniţa on the higher course of the Jiu Valley, Tilişca (Sibiu), Căpîlna and Piatra Craivii to the north-east. At a greater distance fortresses were built at Polovragi (Oltenia) and Bitca Doamnei (Piatra Neamţ in Moldavia).

New types of products were recorded in the ceramic trade, among which were goblets with ornaments in relief, painted vessels and amphorae of the Grecian type. Among vessels made with the wheel were fruit-dishes on a stand, goblets and large vesels for food. In the first century BC the processing of silver was greatly developed. In the special workshops many silver ornaments (bracelets, necklaces) and silver vessels were made. Many of these have been unearthed as treasures, the best known being discovered at Sîncrăieni, Surcea, Lupu (Transylvania); Herăstrău, Merii Goala, Bălăneşti (Wallachia). A remarkable development took place in the field of ferrous metallurgy. There are traces of the extraction, reduction and processing of iron, in various forms, in many Geto-Dacian settlements.

The prints discovered in the Dacian fortress at Tilişca (Sibiu) and those from Ludeşti (Hunedoara) and Braşov prove that, with the constitution of Burebista's state, the Geto-Dacians used a mint taking as a model the Roman republican *denar,* which they copied identically. In the same period they issued a new golden coin with the inscription "Koson", probably the name of a Geto-Dacian king (Koson or Cotison), one of the successors of Burebista, attested by the coins discovered in Transylvania.

The commercial and cultural relations of the Geto-Dacians with the Grecian and Roman world extended and intensified. In Geto-Dacian settlements one can often find ceramic luxury products, metal vessels and jewellery imported from these civilized areas. In the last decades of the second century and at the end of the first century BC, silver coins of Macedonia Prima, Apollonia and Dyrrhachium, of Thasos, and especially *denars* from the Roman world circulated in Dacia. Greek and Roman artists and artisans were brought to Dacia and employed in the building of the great fortresses in the Orăştie Mountains. As a result of these close contacts with the Greek-Roman civilization, some Greek and Latin linguistic elements penetrated into Dacia.

The Geto-Dacian population of that period also had medical knowledge. This is proved by the names of many medicinal herbs preserved in the works of ancient authors and by the discovery of medical pouches. As to the penetration of some philosophical and astronomical ideas, according to Strabo, Zamolxis, who became the supreme god, would have been a disciple of Pythagoras, and Deceneu had travelled through Egypt, where he came into contact with the ideas of ancient philosophy.

The material and spiritual culture of the Geto-Dacians from the Burebista-Decebalus epoch came to the end of its evolution. It reflected faithfully all the economic and political changes that had taken place in the Dacia of that period. One can find here the powerful and rich Thracian tradition in a perfect unity with the progress of those times and the borrowed elements adapted to local needs. The Roman conquest put an end to the general development of the Geto-Dacian civilization, but its essence survived, together with its carriers, until the birth of the Daco-Roman ethno-cultural synthesis and then of the Romanian synthesis.

No place was more important to the Dacians than Sarmizegetusa, the great fortress in the Orăştie Mountains, where, before the Roman conquest, the rulers had their capital. Not only was the fortress of prime political importance but it was also the headquarters of the high priest, containing a number of sanctuaries used for religious purposes, including solar worship and human sacrifice. But did the sanctuaries, which still exist today, serve some purpose other than religious? One who believes that they did is Dr Emil Poenaru, Professor of History at Braşov University, who maintains that one use was the measurement of time. His views are given in an appendix.

2. The Daco-Roman Wars

There was a long and bitter struggle for mastery between the Dacians and the Romans, first one side winning and then the other, until the decisive victory went to the Romans under Emperor Trajan. Following the reign of Augustus, the Dacians of Transylvania were for a long time on the defensive in their mountainous country, but the civil war which raged in the Roman Empire from AD 69 to AD 70 was an occasion for them and the Sarmatians to resume their attacks south of the Danube. Even during Nero's reign, in the winter of AD 67-68, the Roxolan Sarmatians had crossed the Danube into Dobrudja and, taking two auxiliary Roman cohorts by surprise, had slaughtered them. At the close of the year 69 when Aponius had taken his forces to Italy to support Vespasian against Emperor Vitellius the Dacians also went into action, devastating a number of Moesia's districts. Vespasian re-established Roman order along the Danube and persuaded the Dacians to conclude a peace treaty with the Empire, which they observed faithfully for fifteen years. However, after a dispute about their subsidy with Emperor Domitian, the Dacians broke the pact and unexpectedly overran Moesia, inflicting a disastrous defeat on the Romans. Domitian was alarmed and hastened to the Danube. Following the measures taken by him, the invaders were driven back across the river.

In 86 the province of Moesia being considered too big to carry out the military duties devolving upon it, it was divided by Domitian in two. Cornelius Fuscus was put in command of a great army that was to undertake reprisals in Dacia. Sure of victory, Domitian returned to Rome without waiting to see the results of the expedition. Aware of the danger but considering himself too old to face the Romans, Duras, King of the Dacians,

abdicated in favour of Decebalus, son óf Scorilo, who
had ruled before him. Cornelius Fuscus crossed the
Danube on a pontoon bridge in the summer of 87 and
sought to reach the centre of Dacia by the shortest route
which ran through Banat along the Bistra valley towards
Sarmizegetusa, the Dacians' fortress. Fuscus let himself be
drawn into the trap which Decebalus had laid |for him
and with his army met his death in a fearful slaughter
which may have taken place in the Tapae Pass (the Iron
Gates of Transylvania). This was one of the most me-
morable disasters inflicted on the Romans.

Emperor Domitian sent a new army of impressive
proportions against the Dacians. This time the Romans
won a victory but were unable to take full advantage
of it and a compromise peace was concluded in AD 89.
This aroused deep discontent among the senators in
Rome, who were in fierce conflict with Domitian. Consequently, as soon as Trajan ascended the throne in 98,
he made it his aim to suppress the Dacians and the
threat they represented to the Empire. |After detailed
preparations, war was declared by the Romans in the
spring of 101 without any provocation by the Dacian
king. Far from passively awaiting the threat, Decebalus
sought to counterbalance the inferiority of his forces
and the difficulties of his position by wise and audacious
moves. He made an alliance with the Dacian, Sarmatian
and Germanic populations north of the Carpathians, primarily with the Suevian Buri of Slovakia and Maramureș,
and composed a plan under which he meant to take
advantage of Trajan's offensive tactics. When the huge
Roman army had penetrated deep into Transylvania's
Mountains, Decebalus's allies were to spill into Dobrudja
in large numbers and, taking advantage of the poor
Roman defences in those parts, were to make speedily
for the Balkan provinces, intercept Trajan's communica-
tions with the rest of his Empire, striking him from
behind while Decebalus undertook a counter offensive.
Decebalus counted on the Danube being frozen, as was
usual in winter, but in the year of the Roman offensive
the winter was a mild one and this compromised every
thing, as the Roman fleet at Drobeta was not landlocked
by ice and could be used for transporting troops quickly.

At the beginning of the war in the summer of 101
the Romans took the initiative. Two Roman columns
advanced towards Sarmizegetusa, gaining some successes,
but at the height of the winter unexpected news reached

Trajan that Decebalus's allies had crossed into Dobrudja and were attacking the weak auxiliary Roman garrisons along the lower Danube. Leaving behind only sufficient forces to keep the positions that had been won, Trajan took the bulk of his army to Drobeta, where in the early months of 102 he embarked his forces, disembarking at one of the ports of Moesia Inferior. His army gained some successes against the Sarmatians and Dacians in Dobrudja but while this was taking place Decebalus went into action against the Romans in the Transylvanian Mountains, where he gained a victory. However, this was not the spot for the decisive battle of the war. When the main column of Decebalus's allies, the most numerous and strongest, was advancing from northern Dobrudja to the Balkans, Trajan went to meet them with all his forces. The clash that took place on the Adamclisi plateau on the forested steppe of south-western Dobrudja ended in a complete slaughter by the Romans.

The triumph of Emperor Trajan over the Dacians and their allies is marked by a huge monument on the Adamclisi plateau, 161 metres above sea-level, set in a position from which it can be seen from a great distance, as if to signify Rome's strength and to serve as a warning to the tribes defeated in Trajan's wars in AD 101-102. The battle at Adamclisi, in which the Romans lost 3,800 men, an enormous number for a victorious army, was the decisive one of Trajan's campaign. If he had lost — and he nearly did — his prestige would have suffered a crushing blow.

All the Roman forces took part in the battle against Decebalus's allies : auxiliaries, legionaries, Pretorians, the Emperor's personal guard, the Roman war engines. The mutilated text of Dio Cassius, referring to this battle, says : "Trajan saw many wounded among his men and killed many of the enemy, and as bandages were insufficient he is said not to have spared his own clothes, which he tore into strips to bind the wounds ; for those who had died in battle he ordered that an altar be raised and services to their memory be officiated every year."

This monument, originally 40 metres high and dedicated to Mars, the god of war, had on top the figure of a Roman soldier in full armour. Erected in 106-9, it originally contained a mausoleum to shelter the remains of a high officer who fell during the battle — *praefectus castrorum* — and an altar, on the walls of which the names of the 3,800 soldiers were carved in stone. During the following centuries the monument became a ruin, a massive pile of stones and mortar, and even the reason why it was erected was forgotten. During the Turkish rule in Dobrudja the monument was given the name *Adamclisi,* man's church, because the existing core was thought to resemble the cupola of a Christian church. Research, in which the Romanian scholar Grigore Tocilescu was a leading figure, led to the rediscovery of the purposes of the monument and eventually to plans for its restoration. The most valuable features were the metopes, rectangular sculptured stone slabs in circular arrangements, showing scenes from Roman campaigns and from the battle at Adamclisi. There were originally fifty-four metopes, but some have been lost, others destroyed, and there is even one on display in the archaeological museum in Istanbul, where it was taken in the middle of the last century. Fortunately it has been possible to reconstruct some lost metopes from descriptions of them handed down by earlier travellers. Some of the slabs were retrieved from the surrounding countryside, graveyards and households. The metopes, which had an average height of 1.58 metres and a width of 1.61 metres, showed the Romans wearing helmets and coats of mail while the Dacians rarely carried weapons and fought almost naked. Some metopes feature Dacian civil refugees — men, women and children — and captured Dacians, flanked by Roman soldiers.

I visited the reconstructed monument with Dr Adrian Rădulescu, Director of the Museum of History and Archaeology at Constanţa. This involved a drive of 65 kilometres along the highway to Bucharest and then down a side road. The monument, gleaming in its newness, dominates the countryside. What we see here are copies of the original metopes and of most of its other features. For the originals you have to visit the museum in the village at Adamclisi, where, in addition to the metopes, there is the figure which originally stood on top of the monument and the altar stone with the names of the soldiers who fell in battle inscribed on it.

Immediately after the Adamclisi victory Trajan re-embarked his forces, sailed up the Danube and returned to the Transylvanian Mountains to resume his advance towards Sarmizegetusa. Operations had to start from scratch as during his absence the positions occupied the year before had been lost to Decebalus. At the close of AD 102 a solemn peace was concluded which lasted two years. When the war was resumed, it was fought in the Orăştie Mountains in the spring and summer of 106. All the citadels on the mountaintops were conquered one after the other with great difficulty, and Sarmizegetusa itself was finally surrounded. Opposing the Roman assaults with epic gallantry, the capital fell only when its water supplies were exhausted and its last defenders had died from thirst. Decebalus stabbed himself with his curved dagger to avoid being taken prisoner. After the fall of Sarmizegetusa Regia, the Romans took every measure to ensure that this sacred place of the Dacians should be denied to them in the future. They deported the population of the region to other parts of the country, destroyed the religious sanctuaries, and for a long time kept a garrison in the conquered citadel. In 106, the year of victory, Dacia was proclaimed a Roman province. Colonia Ulpia Trajana, subsequently to be called Sarmizegetusa, was to be the main city of the new province ; it was thirty-five miles away from Decebalus's Sarmizegetusa in the Orăştie Mountains.

Among the chain of fortresses built in the second century by the victorious Romans was one, Tropaeum Traiani, within sight of Trajan's monument at Adamclisi. At first sight, viewed from the east gate, it seems to be just a handful of ruins, with a few local people putting cement on crumbling walls, but as I walked with Dr Rădulescu down the road running through the middle of the fortress the extent of the stronghold, covering 150,000 square metres, became apparent. This fortress, which was built on the site of a Geto-Dacian settlement, was destroyed by migratory tribes such as the Goths in the middle of the third century and again, after rebuilding, by the Avars at the end of the sixth century. In this century the fortress had been a religious centre. Near the east gate were the remains of two small basilicas of the Byzantine type, one on each side of the road, where marks made by chariots and carts were still visible, and nearer the west gate two other small basilicas once stood, with a fifth one outside the fortress. As I stood with Dr Rădulescu on the site of an altar, he pointed out behind it a small cavity which had once held the remains of a saint. What impressed me in this fortress was the small scale of everything, churches, houses and shops, as if all aspects of a Roman settlement had to be compressed within the protecting walls which might at any time be threatened by warlike hordes. Even the hall with its remains of columns near the west gate where the senate once met could not have accommodated many people. If the east gate seemed as if it led to a handful of ruins, a totally different impression was conveyed at the western gate, where walls have been rebuilt to their original size. The arch of the west gate has still to be restored and a covered way provided for the shops which once stood at this end of the fortress.

Dr Rădulescu said that excavations started here in 1882, and every year between twenty and seventy people worked on the site, with one archaeologist to every ten workers He estimated that the restoration of the fortress could take another twenty to thirty years.

No part of Romania provides a more fascinating mixture of races than Dobrudja, known in Roman times as Moesia Inferior and since the fourth century as Scythia Minor. Among the Greek colonies on the shores of Romania the oldest and most thoroughly investigated is Histria, the fortress built by colonists from Miletus on the Sinoe lake, which in ancient, times was a large gulf, Halmyris. The name of Histria was derived from *"Istros"*, the Greek name for the Danube, the town being set up in the vicinity of its mouths. According to a written source, Histria was founded in 657-656 BC but the earliest material found there dates from the end of the seventh century BC. For twelve hundred years, until the seventh century AD, Histria played a significant role as a port and economic centre, but with the passing of time the place was surrounded by sand, ships could no longer cast anchor there, and trade was diverted to Tomis (modern Constanţa, Romania's largest port). The citadel was gradually abandoned and the once celebrated centre of Greek culture and trade was ruined by migratory hordes of Avars and Slavs. The site was re-discovered as the result of researches by the historian and archaeologist Vasile Pârvan in 1914-16 and 1921-27. The researches, started by Pârvan, who has been described as the father of Romanian archaeology, are still being continued and have been expanded.

Although Histria is now but a ruined site, Mangalia, as the old Greek city of Callatis is now called, is a modern town and spa centre. Important excavations have taken place there. One site is at Albeşti, near Callatis, where excavations have brought to light evidence of the links between Greeks and Dacians. Some of the more important finds are in the archaeological museum

in the town, but one of the interesting discoveries from
this district, is the body of a woman found in 1972 near
Callatis, is in the archaeological museum at Constanța.
This woman, who was rather tall and very rich, judging by the possessions buried with her, including a golden
crown, died about AD 147 at the age of forty-seven or
eight, from the effects of lead poisoning. Analysis
of the skin and bones has revealed that she used
powder made from lead. When she admired herself in the
mirror made of bronze and gold, also found in the tomb,
she could not have realized that her vanity was slowly
causing her death.

One of the most dramatic finds ever made in Constanța, and displayed in the museum there, is the contents of a pit unearthed at a depth of seven metres on
the site of the former railway station near the archaeological park. This pit contained twenty-four statues of
deities and bas-reliefs from various temples buried for
safety in the third or fourth centuries to protect them
from the Christians, according to Dr Rădulescu. The
deities include a life-size statuary group, Fortuna-
Pontos, of Carrara marble. It represents the goddess
Fortuna standing and carrying the horn of plenty in
her left hand. The right hand, in which she was carrying the sceptre, was probably lost in antiquity. At her
feet stands the little figure of Pontos — the god of the
Black Sea — naked and leaning on a boat, wearing a
crown in imitation of the lay-out of the city's precinct
walls with its main gates. Both the goddess and the
god were patrons of ancient Tomis. Also shown here is
the *glykon*, a household god with the body of a serpent,
the mouth of a lamb or a meek dog, a man's ears, long
hair and a lion's tail. The *glykon*, dating from the second
or third century AD, was known only from coins until
this one was discovered, and visitors have come from
all over the world to see it. No other has since been
found. Also of great interest is a double representation
of Nemesis, the goddess of retributive justice, holding a
graduated measuring instrument similar to a rule which
she used to measure the good and bad deeds. These
treasures came to light when a site was being excavated
for the construction of a block of flats.

It has been established that at Tomis, on the very
jetty of the ancient harbour, a great sculpture workshop
existed. Ships from the south carried as ballast big
marble blocks which were unloaded on the quay, where

numerous sculptors and stonecutters started work on
the spot, turning them into useful pieces to decorate
public buildings, squares, palaces or private dwellings.

Adjoining the archaeological museum is a Roman
edifice with a mosaic floor which in antiquity comprised the largest mosaic floor in the world (two thousand square metres, a hundred metres long, twenty metres wide). The Board for Historical Monuments has
built a concrete roof and glass walls above and around
the mosaic-floored terrace, but this has only a protec-
tive role and has nothing in common with the original
aspect of the edifice, which seems to have been roof-
less. The new roof does not give a true indication of
the original proportion and size of the building that
once stood here, facing the ancient harbour.

Constanţa has its own archaeological park in Repub-
licii Boulevard containing more than a hundred massive monuments : pediments, capitals, inscriptions,
columns and sarcophagi. A series of *pithoi-dolia*, big jars
of baked clay for storing lignite (a thousand litres), show
the development of economic life in towns and villages.
The receptacles, fashioned and fired on the spot, were
also used to store grain, drinking-water, wine, salt fish,
meat and other foods. In the middle of the park are
an immense marble architrave and four large marble
blocks from the sculpture workshop discovered on the
quays.

More than five thousand inscriptions relating to Dacians and Romans have been discovered in Dobrudja,
but during the Ottoman occupation some were taken to
Europe, ending up in the Louvre in Paris and the
British Museum in London. Among the inscriptions were
those found on tombstones, in the homes of citizens, on
milestones and on altars. Some inscriptions show that
soldiers went from Dacia to Britain (Britannia) and
returned. Dr. Rădulescu said that we had to rely on
these inscriptions for records from the past because
paper perished in the damp sea air. One document from
the fourth century BC found in Callatis in 1959 dis-
integrated when produced in the air.

From an inscription discovered on the seashore at
Histria we learn of complaints of peasants from the
village Choradageis against their being subjected to
heavy duties in keeping the roads in good repair — it
was naturally the coastal road which was always in a
bad state. They demanded to be exempt from such du-

ties, as were the people of the village of Laicos Pyrgos. Both requests were granted.

While during the Roman epoch the inscriptions were elaborate works of sculpture, in the fourth to sixth centuries they were more simple, in a rustic style and less artistic ; many were just sketches or Christian symbols. However, their written content provided extremely valuable information. Among the more important historical data concerning the life in the region are the names of the military units at Ulmetum and Tomis, the lancers and archers, the name of the lawyer in Callatis written in Greek — Symplicius, and the name of a vicar of Odessos engraved on a stone in Tomis, and the reference at Axiopolis to Gibastes and his daughter Anthusa. Inscriptions in Tomis also attest the names of prelates, such as that of Timotei Paternus and that of a keeper of St. John's Church (unidentified so far). There is also much information about people's names with an almost equal number of Greek and Latin names as well as those of Thracian-Getian-Dacian origin (Decebalus, Kyndeas, Dinias etc.), Gothic (Gibastes), Turanian (Atala, Tzeenink), from Asia Minor (Entolios, Focas, Thecla), all this being proof of the close contacts between the province of Scythia and the neighbouring or remote regions.

The Christian inscriptions in Dobrudja mainly reflect funerary practices, while the sculptural elements reveal a concern for beauty, especially in Christian public edifices. Symbols such as the fish, the dove, the cross, either simple or monogrammatic, the rosette etc are frequent. Capitals (the top or head of columns) among others, the Theodosian type, covered by geometric, vegetal or zoomorphic decorations met everywhere. Remarkable by its artistic value is a capital with rams' heads, discovered at Callatis, which by its opulent ornamentation predicts the late Baroque style.

In 1912 an accidental find at Malaia Perscepina, in the Ukraine near Paltewa, revealed a hoard containing among other things a silver tray of Byzantine craftsmanship that had an inscription bearing the name of Tomis. This tray, now in the Hermitage Museum in Leningrad, is shaped as a discus and is decorated with splendid vegetal and zoomorphic motifs ; it ranks among the most valable treasures of the metropolitan seat of Tomis which at the time of the Emperor Anastasius consisted of fourteen bishoprics and was headed by Paternus, the bishop who in 520 signed the documents of the Ecumenical Council of Constantinople. It is generally accepted that the tray was manufactured in Byzantium but there is the possibility that it may have been a product of the art of Tomis, which was considerably developed, even at the beginning of the sixth century.

The existence of the bishopric at Tomis and the inherent survival of the city itself during troubled times have been proved not only by literary sources but also by archaeological discoveries. Thus, on the floor of a big basilica in Tomis, burnt clay pottery was found with characteristics of the Roman-Byzantine tradition. Dated in the seventh century and at the beginning of the eighth century, they are the products of the local population who took shelter in the ruined basilicas. Similar pottery has been found at Callatis and in many other centres. Archaeological investigations in Dobrudja include tens of settlements which yielded many pieces of pottery enabling scholars to make a distinction between certain types dated before the tenth century and others after that time. Complete vases, such as those found at Rasova (painted with red ochre), Camena, Murighiol, Teliţa, together with those which came from the excavations at Axiopolis, Capidava, Dinogeţia etc, are sound proof of the continuity of the Romanian population up to the date of the reorganization of the Byzantine administration in Dobrudja in 971. Dr. Rădulescu told me that the best evidence for the continuity of the Romanian people is found in Dobrudja, which between 271 and 639 remained under Roman domination.

Quite frequently graphic signs appear on the earthen or stone vases : Greek, Cyrillic, Glagolitic and Latin letters. On a stone found at Axiopolis (Cernavoda), now lost, Vasile Pârvan read the name Voislav, written with Greek and Slav letters, a testimony to Romanian cultural manifestations in the ninth century. Another proof of this culture is a jar found at Capidava which bears an inscription in Greek. At the end of the letters appears the name Petre, a common one in the Danube valley. This is not part of a religious prayer because there is no religious hymn devoted to St. Peter but only to SS Petru and Pavel, celebrated together in the Orthodox Church. The exclusive use of the Greek alphabet in the inscription on this jar reveals the strong Byzantine influence which preceded the Slavonic one and gained many adherents among the Romanians. A limestone block discovered in 1959 at Mircea Vodă, in the Carasu Valley, bore the name of Jupan Dimitrie, a local feudal nobleman who in 943 probably took part in the fights in that area with Magyars, Pechenegs and Russians. The inscription is in Cyrillic letters which gradually replaced the Byzantine alphabet in Dobrudja.

The Byzantine Empire returned to the Danube in the last third of the tenth century. Stability was ensured by the numerous Danubian fortresses and towns which were economic, cultural and religious centres, rebuilt or newly built by the Byzantines. One of these fortresses situated on Pacuiul lui Soare Island ("Island of the Sun") in the Constanța district represents such a river fortress raised by the Empire in 971-6 in the immediate neighbourhood of the capital of the Byzantine territories from the lower Danube, situated at Dorostolon-Silistra. Intensive archaeological research has been carried out on this island for the past twenty-five years, about twenty workers under the supervision of two or three archaeologists being engaged, according to Dr. Rădulescu.

Byzantine administrative, economic, cultural or military centres, dating from the end of the tenth century and from the eleventh and twelfth centuries, have also been searched at Capidava in the Constanța district and at Dinogetia Isaccea (old Roman Noviodunum), Nufaru or Enisala, all of them in the Tulcea district. In the wine-growing district of Murfatlar, near Constanța, researchers recently found a monastic complex with inscribed rocks, dating from about 1000 AD and consisting of several small churches and dwellings, with numerous inscriptions and religious symbols linked to the return of the Empire in the north of the Balkan Peninsula. The consolidation of Byzantine influence was also felt at that time in the vast territories of the northern part of the Danube.

More than a hundred sculptures and bas-reliefs have been discovered on the sites of ancient Tomis, Callatis and their surroundings, and more than three hundred Tanagra statuettes, as well as numerous treasures of coins minted in the workshops of Histria, Callatis and Tomis. In the storerooms of the Constanța museum more than ten thousand archaeological exhibits are classified according to scientific criteria and supplemented by reference cards which include data referring to their finding, identification, similarities and so on. Some of the items in the museum are unique. For instance, a sundial of the second century AD, discovered at Cumpana village, ten kilometres south of Constanţa, which in antiquity was a rural settlement or a Roman villa, is the only one of its kind found in Romania, and a bronze Scythian cauldron of the fifth century BC, unearthed at Castelu village, in the Carasu valley near Medgidia in 1960, is only one of three discovered in Romania. Such cauldrons were used by the Scythian tribes for boiling their food.

Archaeology has played a crucial part in bringing to light evidence for the continuity of the Romanian people, Dr Rădulescu said. Twenty archaeologists work in the museum at Constanţa, ten others in the museum at Tulcea, the gateway town to the Danube delta, and in the season between ten and twelve come to the district from Bucharest to help with excavations in which six hundred workers are engaged, all supervised by archaeologists.

About twenty sites in the district are worked yearly. The most important is Medgidia, a strong fortress from the fourth century BC to the first century of our era. Excavations are still taking place at Albeşti, Sacidava, Axiopolis, Capidava, Dinogeţia, Noviodunum, Aegysius, Tropaeum Traiani, Argamum, Histria, Tomis and Callatis.

Cemeteries are also being excavated at some of these places, for the evidence of the past yielded by the contents of tombs buried with their owner. In Callatis (Mangalia), for instance, numerous offerings to the gods — clay pots, coins, jewels, statuettes — were found buried in vaults and graves. These objects have been unearthed from thousands of graves, following archaeological investigations or occasional diggings.

The Byzantine domination set up again at the Danube by the end of the tenth century, which extended, in certain periods, also to north of the Danube, was maintained during the eleventh and twelfth centuries. Discoveries such as those at Capidava, where researchers found ceramics with inscriptions scratched in the paste, attest the presence of Romanians in the towns along the Danube. The main mass of the descendants of the eastern part of the Roman Empire, the so-called "Balchan Wallach" (Balkan Wallachians), at that time lived mainly in the mountain zones in the centre of the Balkan Peninsula. Detached, after the sixth century, from the unitary mass of the Latin population and pushed by the Slavs, according to written sources, south of the sheltered regions, by the end of the twelfth century they were at the head of the movement which led to the creation, in the north-east of present Bulgaria, of a new state, the Romanian-Bulgarian tsardom of the Asăneşti dynasty with the capital at Tîrnovo.

Until the middle of the thirteenth century, during the big Mongol invasion, the Asăneşti state represented the main political force in the north of the Balkan Peninsula. Later the Dobrudjan despotate — the despot who ruled over the area between the Danube and the Black Sea in the fourteenth century was named Dobrotici, hence Dobrudji or Dobrudja — was detached from it because of the intensification of Byzantine efforts to recover the former imperial territories, from the time of the Palaeologus dynasty. Archaeological discoveries, such as those at Niculiţel in the north of Dobrudja or at Vadu at the seaside (Constanţa district), attest the unity of the culture and civilization of the Romanian territories situated north and south of the Danube. They explain also the inclusion of Dobrudja, by the end of the fourteenth century, in the boundaries of the Romanian country ruled by Prince Mircea the Old, one of the greatest rulers in the history of Romania. From the next century, as a result of conditions created by the progress of the Turkish offensive in this part of Europe, Dobrudja was to be included for four centuries in the Ottoman Empire without modifying deeply the ethnic and demographical characteristics of the region.

The earliest evidence testifying to the relations between the present-day territory of Romania and the areas in the Near East inhabited nowadays by Muslim peoples dates back to remote neolithic times. This evidence is the pre-cuneiform inscriptions on terracotta tablets, discovered at Tărtăria, a village near Sebeş in Transylvania — these inscriptions are the earliest examples of handwriting so far found in Romania — similar to those found in Mesopotamia. Very close links with the Near East are attested again by the archaeological monuments belonging to the Iron Age. In Babadag, an important town between Constanţa and Tulcea, there are elements dating from the seventh century BC whose origins must be sought in Anatolia ; later on, in the fourth century AD, the Geto-Thracian treasures were characterized by an iconography and a style possessing many elements of Iranian origin which were likely to have been brought by the Phrygians related to them who occupied the very centre of Anatolia and also by the Persian armies and merchants after Darius, who in 514 BC conquered Thracia.

In the period of Roman rule, troops of Oriental and Maghrib soldiers — from Syria and the city of Palmyra, as well as Moors — are known to have been stationed in Dacia. That is why on many Daco-Roman monuments in Ulpia Trajana, Apulum, Drobeta and Tomis we can see Oriental and African gods side by side with Greek, Roman and Thracian ones. Such are Jupiter, Minerva, Venus, Mars, the Thracian Rider, Dionysus, Aesculapius and the Oriental or African gods Dea Syria, Jupiter/ Dolichenus, Dei Mauri, the national gods of the Berbers, Sol Invictus, the god of Baalbek and others. A little later, in the early Christian period, we find a Syrian-type basilica at Callatis as well as stamped ceramics, a feature peculiar to the production centres in Syria and Palestine.

Very few ceramics have been preserved in Muslim settlements but some beautiful specimens are to be found in the Oriental Art Museum at Babadag and in the "Barbu Slătineanu" Comparative Art Museum in Bucharest.

The Dobrudja area has not attracted the same amount of attention from historians hostile to Romania's claim to continuity of race as have the other parts of Romania, because from here, south of the Danube, the evidence of Roman influence following the departure of Aurelian is so strong. It developed from here to the north. Archaeologists, amateur and professional, will find Constanța a good starting place for a visit to Romania because of the wealth of Greek and Roman remains as well as those of the Dacians and Muslims.

3. After the Romans

The establishment of the Romans at the Danube, as far back as the reign of Emperor Augustus, generated many conflicts between Dacians and Romans, starting with simple incursions on both sides of the Danube and ending with the great wars in the reigns of Decebalus and Trajan. Ancient sources registered the first incursion in 15 BC against the south Danubian Roman domination. Two years later Agrippa repelled a Dacian attack in Pannonia, the area covered by present-day Hungary, and in 10-9 BC a new attack was repelled by M. Vinicius in the same province. In AD 6-9 the Dacians, with the Sarmatians, penetrated Moesia, and in 11-12 Cornelius Lentulus attacked the Dacians on the left bank of the Danube.

In order to weaken the power of the Geto-Dacians the Romans proceeded to remove the north Danubian population to south of the river. This was done in AD 9 by Aelius Catus and in Nero's time by Plantius Sylvanus Aelianus. From now on, the economic, political and religious power of the Geto-Dacians was centred in intra-Carpathian Dacia (Transylvania). Moreover, Roman actions were concerned almost exclusively with this part of Dacia, known for its riches in gold. Because of the new situation, political changes took place. Rome eventually triumphed. According to the writer Joanes Lydos, the Romans took out of Dacia huge riches, including 165,000 kilos of gold and 331,000 kilos of silver. In memory of this victory that famous monument, the Column of Trajan, was erected in Rome. Here, in scenes carved in marble, the climax of the two Daco-Roman wars is represented.

Immediately after the conquest one part of the territory of Dacia, formed of Transylvania, Banat and Oltenia, became a Roman province of imperial rank under the name of Dacia Province. The free Dacians, left outside the new Roman frontiers, inhabited the territories of Crişana, Maramureş and a part of Wallachia and Moldavia. The defence of the province was secured by the XIII Legion Gemina stationed at Apulum and later by the V Legion Macedonica stationed at Potaissa (Turda), as well as by a large number of auxiliary troops — in all, about seventy thousand soldiers. Among the defence lines several Roman camps were built.

The Romans founded in Dacia a large number of cities, most of them on the ruins of the old Geto-Dacian settlements, maintaining their original names. Among them were the capital of the province, Ulpia Traiana Augusta Dacia, Sarmizegetusa (Hunedoara district), Apulum (Alba Iulia), Napoca (Cluj), Potaissa (Turda) and Porollisum (Moigrad). The cities founded in Lower Dacia were Romula-Malva (Drobeta-Turnu Severin) and Dierna (Orşova) and, in Banat, Tibiscum.

According to the Latin writer Eutropius, for the organization of the new province Trajan brought a large number of colonists to Dacia from all over the Roman Empire because "Dacia lost its men in the long war of Decebalus." Julian the Apostate attributed to Trajan the affirmation that, "He destroyed the Getae, who were the greatest warriors of all times." According to Joanes Lydos, a great number of prisoners were brought to Rome, and a part of the population took refuge in the unoccupied regions of Dacia.

Using this information of the ancient writers and without an analysis of the texts and without proper judgement, the Romanians claim, some historians have asserted that the wars for the conquest of Dacia led to the extermination of all the Geto-Dacian population. A critical review of the literary tradition does not allow us to speak about anything other than natural human losses in conflicts such as the ancient wars. There have never been wars that led to complete extermination, not even of the army. The wars in question could not have resulted in the entire civilian population of a nation as large as that of the Geto-Dacians being exterminated. Also, the Latin historian Dio Cassius, one of the ancient writers who lived in a period of time closer to these events than most other commentators, says that during the second war "many Dacians joined Trajan" and does not mention anything about the extermination of the Geto-Dacian population. In the opinion of most historians, some scenes on Trajan's Column represent acts of obedience of the Dacian population. Other scenes show the refugee Dacians returning to their own places. The extermination of the entire Geto-Dacian population would not have been in the spirit and the interest of the policy of the Roman Empire, which needed the local population to exploit the riches of the soil and the subsoil of the new province.

Dacia was the province where, after Trajan, the Romans recruited the largest number of troops for the needs of the Empire. There were Dacian military corps in Syria, Britannia, Moesia and Dalmatia. The formation of these troops suggests that even from Trajan's epoch there was a significant number of young men in Dacia. This refutes the statements of Eutropius concerning the total absence of men after the two wars, and the theory of the so-called extermination of the Geto-Dacian population.

Among the inscriptions discovered in Dacia there are those in the Latin language which contain Thraco-Dacian names. Because of the names of various people mentioned in these inscriptions we have to accept the existence of Romanized Dacians as a result of the right of the original population, including Dacians married to Romans, to become Roman citizens.

The maintaining of the old place-names and waterways of Dacia is also due to the original Dacians. The Romans took over directly from the Dacian population the names of the main rivers: Danubius from the old Dacian Donaris, Argessos-Ordessos (Argeş), Alutus (Olt), Maris (Mureş), Pyretus-Porata (Prut), Samus (Someş). Most of the cities of Dacia as well as some new settlements kept the original Geto-Dacian names. Among the best known in Transylvania are Sarmizegetusa, Apulum, Napoca, Potaissa, Tibiscum, Porolissum, Archidava, Ampelum and Alburnus, and in Oltenia Drobeta, Dierna and Sucidava. In Lower Moesia (Dobrudja) most known cities have names with typical Geto-Dacian endings : Capidava, Sucidava, Argedava, Sacidava. It is believed that the word *dava* was used by the Geto-Dacians to denote a city-seat, the centre of a political unit or union of tribes.

Linguistic studies made by specialists have led to the identification in the Romanian language of 170 words of Dacian origin in different fields. This represents one of the inheritances of the Dacian and Daco-Roman conti-

nuity during several centuries as a result of the persistence of the Dacian ethnic element.

Among the archaeological discoveries directly related
to the problem of Dacian continuity is a group of Dacian
settlements such as those of Slimnic and Rosia (Sibiu
district in Transylvania), where traces of material culture show that they were inhabited without interruption
from the second century BC to the second and third
centuries AD. In these archaeological complexes one can
find an effective and uninterrupted Dacian presence
from the period before the conquest of Dacia and during
the Roman period.

Other archaeological discoveries, probably the most
representative in proving the persistence of Dacian occupation in the province, are related to the Daco-Roman
cultural aspect, such as the discoveries at Soporul de
Cîmpie-Obreja (Transylvania) and Locusteni (Oltenia).
These relate to a new cultural aspect which dates from
the second and third centuries AD when the Geto-Dacian
tradition was predominant. In the settlements and cemeteries ceramics specific to Geto-Dacian culture and the
rite of cremation appeared, continuing the old local tradition. Such discoveries were made in several places in
the provinces concerned and show that the population
was uniformly spread and that it was quite strong and
numerous enough to be able to affirm itself from an
ethnic and cultural point of view.

Most of the discoveries of this kind are concentrated
in Transylvania. In addition to the big cemeteries of
Soporul de Cîmpie (Cluj district) and that of Obreja
(Alba district), where one can find an important settlement with the same cultural characteristics, researchers
have made similar discoveries in over 40 localities such
as at Alba Iulia, Zlatna (Alba district), Caşolţ (Sibiu district), Cernatu de Jos (Covasna district), Cinciş and Ighiu
(Hunedoara district), Cristeşi Lechinţa and Sighişoara
(Mureş district).

These archaeological investigations proved that the
original Dacian element penetrated even the main Roman
centres of Dacia. Traces of Dacian culture were discovered, without exception, in all the cities, in Roman
military camps and in the civilian settlements in Dacia.

The evidence for the persistence of Dacian occupation
under the Romans is also strengthened by discoveries of
coins. An analysis of the monetary treasures found in
Transylvania, as in the rest of the province, established

that the process of accumulation of them started in the first century AD and continued during the Roman epoch in the second and third centuries. The many owners of these treasures belonged to the Geto-Dacian society which collected coins before and after the Roman conquest. Among the monetary treasures of Transylvania are those discovered at Alba Iulia, Alecuş, Dimbău, Hunedoara, Jeledinţi, Lăpuşnic, Reghin, Tibodu, and Vişea. In each of these places Roman imperial coins from the first to the third century have been found.

Archaeological discoveries, as arguments for the continuity of the race in Roman Dacia, are much more numerous and varied than those mentioned, and I will give details of some later in the book. They are not limited to a certain region or a single type of settlement. On the contrary, Dacian cultural traces can be found in all the territory of the province, more numerous in rural areas but also to be found in urban and military centres. When we add the archaeological proof to the inscriptions discovered and to linguistic sources, we have a clear image of the continuity of the Dacian population and may conclude that the Dacian population went on representing the main ethnic element of the province even after the conquest of the country.

The persistence of the Dacians in the province shows only one aspect of the continuity of the race in the entire territory of pre-Roman Dacia. It is clear that in the non-occupied areas the Dacian population remained, continuing to develop further its own political and cultural life. The population of the free Dacians is mentioned many times in written sources, and further confirmation is provided by archaeological discoveries. The presence of the free Dacians in the western and north-western parts of Transylvania (the regions of Crişana and Maramureş, outside the Roman boundaries) was identified by a local cultural aspect known under the name of Sîntana (Arad district) and Medieşu Aurit (Satu Mare district). Here researchers have found an uninterrupted Dacian inhabitancy during the fourth to sixth centuries AD. The main characteristics of this cultural aspect are the traditional ones, especially represented by the rite of cremation specific to the old world of the Geto-Dacians, and by a series of ceramics known from the pre-Roman epoch. A similar situation existed in the other regions of the free Dacians, Wallachia and Moldavia, where also the material culture of the second and third centuries

AD is represented by an important number of settlements and cremation cemeteries, in essence the old Geto-Dacian civilization developed in new conditions. It is clear that between the material and spiritual culture of the free Dacians and that of the Dacians from the Roman-occupied province there are similarities in all respects, proof of the Geto-Dacian ethnic unity and of the continuity of the race on the entire territory of Dacia. All this demonstrates that even after the conquest of Dacia, in the province as well as in the regions not occupied by the Romans, the basic ethnic element was the old Geto-Dacian population which, it is claimed, was the basis for the formation of the Romanian people.

In addition to the continuity, the Romanization was an essential element in the formation of the Romanian people. Aspects of the same process, the continuity and the Romanization, took place simultaneously, conditioning each other, until the achievement of the Daco-Roman synthesis.

The analysis of written sources and of the results of archaeological, epigraphical and linguistic researches allow us to appreciate that Romanization was a real, effective and complex process which took place over a long period and which did not limit itself to the province. Although it was a slower process, it was extended in time to the whole local population inside the boundaries of pre-Roman Dacia.

The change of Dacia into a province of the Empire created a favourable frame for the development of an effective and systematic Romanization of the Geto-Dacian population. In order to organize and exploit the province, many colonists, Roman citizens and pilgrims, merchants, mining specialists and soldiers were brought there. Such a situation caused the Byzantine Zonaros to write: "Even from the conquest of Dacia, the Dacians and their province became Romans." Used in all fields of activity and in the mining of Dacia's riches, the Roman colonists were in direct contact with the original population of the Dacians. The permanent living together of the two ethnic elements encouraged and accelerated the appropriation by the Dacians of Roman culture and the Latin language.

An important role in the Romanization process was played by the Roman army transferred to Dacia for the defence of the boundaries. From inscriptions and other written sources we know that a great many troops, estimated at about seventy thousand soldiers, organized in twenty cavalry corps (*alae*), forty-eight infantry troops (*cohortae*) and sixteen to seventeen auxiliary formations were stationed in Dacia, especially in Transylvania. Many camps and fortresses were built for these troops. Civilian settlements developed around them as a result of the establishment of the veterans in Dacia at the end of their military service. Among the carriers of Roman culture and possessors of the Latin language there were the Dacians recruited for the armies of other provinces of the Roman Empire who returned completely Romanized after twenty-five years of military service. Life in urban centres also contributed to the Romanization of the Dacian population. More "cities" were founded in Dacia than in any other province of the Empire. All these "cities", centres of civilization, with a large number of Roman citizens, represented places for spreading the Latin culture and language to the whole province. A similar role in the process of Romanization, but not to the same extent, was played by the other types of Roman settlement, such as small towns, Customs stations and Roman farms (*villae*) spread all over Dacia.

The organization of the exploitation of the soil and especially of the riches below the earth, namely the rich gold mines of Transylvania, needed a large labour force, recruited from the specialized colonists, as well as from the local population. Used for less specialized activities, especially in the fields, the work of the Dacians was a part of the general plan for exploitation of the province, and this suggests a direct and permanent contact with the Roman colonists and administration.

An indication of the extent and depth of the process of Romanization is provided by almost three thousand Latin inscriptions discovered in Dacia. Most come from the military and urban centres, as well as from the mining regions. So far, only 230 inscriptions have been discovered in the countryside. This provides proof of the penetration of the Latin language, even to those Dacians who were engaged in farming. Latin became the language of the whole population of the province. The common interests of the Roman administration, of the colonists and of the Dacian population, in the organization and exploitation of the natural resources of Dacia, required the use of a single official and unitary language which could only be Latin.

Archaeological researches have made a substantial contribution to the demonstration of the Romanization process in Dacia. The results show not only a very large spread of Roman culture and way of life in the entire territory of the province but also that Dacians and Romans lived together in all the settlements in Dacia. In the centres where there was a Dacian majority one can also find, beside the old local elements, the presence of the influences of Roman civilization. At the same time, in the Roman "cities", camps and civilian settlements around them, one can frequently find traces of Dacian traditional culture and of the Dacian presence in the urban centres and of their participation, together with the colonists, in the various activities linked to the organization and exploitation of the province.

The intertwining of the two ethnic groups and of the two civilizations in the 170 years of Roman domination led to the formation of a unitary Daco-Roman culture and population. Over a century and a half of the effects of Roman domination did not mean, as some critics have objected, that this was too short a period to achieve the process of Romanization. Examples offered by other provinces from the West (Gallia and Hispania), where it is estimated that the process of Romanization took place in a shorter period of time, demonstrate, with the other arguments given above, the lack of grounds for such a belief Moreover, it should not be forgotten that in Dacia some elements specific to the beginning of the process of Romanization appeared almost two centuries before the conquest and that the process itself could not be expected to stop after Aurelian's withdrawal.

Romanization was not limited to the population of the province. Although under different conditions, it also included gradually and over a long period the free Dacians outside the Roman boundaries. A differentiation which takes into consideration the intensity of the process refers especially to the period when the Romans settled in Dacia. During the rest of the time, before the conquest and after Aurelian's withdrawal, conditions were more or less the same for the entire Geto-Dacian population.

During the reign of Emperor Aurelian, according to some historians in AD 271, to others in 274-5, Dacia ceased to be a Roman province. Ancient sources, quite late, of the fourth to sixth centuries AD (Aurelius

Victor Eutropius and Rufius Festus, *Historia Augusta,* Jordanes), which speak about the loss or the leaving of Dacia, are quite brief and are not clear. None of them offers exact information about the immediate reasons for the nature of the abandonment of the province. However, we should bear in mind that the migrations during the previous century had filled the plains around this Carpathian bastion with numerous warlike populations, and this had totally changed the balance of power along the Danube. The Empire, now without internal resources as a result of the crisis it had undergone, had to economize its forces by cutting down the long perimeter of Trajan's province and resuming the defensive line along the Danube. Under the new conditions, Dacia was of no use to the Empire from a military point of view. It was no longer efficient in defending the Danubian frontier ; on the contrary, it jeopardized it, disjointing the boundary and depriving it of important forces required within. The great barbarian forces skirted Dacia fearlessly to attack the provinces of Illyricum and Moesia. Withdrawal from Dacia did not mean that the strategic position before Trajan was being reverted to. Even without Roman forces, Dacia, with most of its population Romanized, did not consider itself separated from Rome, and the Empire was still powerful enough not to allow a new enemy force, such as that of the Dacians of old, to overrun the territory of its former province.

Aurelian evacuated Dacia in good order, unhampered by the barbarians who had been beaten and reduced to a state of peace all along the Lower Danube. The forces of the province crossed to the right bank of the river: Legion XIII Gemina occupied the *castrum* at Ratiaria (Archar) while Legion V Macedonica returned to its old garrison at Oescus (Ghighen). The administrative officials were withdrawn simultaneously with the army and were followed by the rich and by a part of the townspeople who were settled between the Danube and the Balkans. On these territories a new province was founded. It was named Dacia, not only as a consolation to Roman prestige but also because its army, its administrative machinery and the foremost social elements of the population were identical with those of the province that had been abandoned. The new Dacia lay along the Danube contiguously with what had formerly been Dacia Inferior. Probably the Dacia of Aurelian was already from the beginning divided in two provinces which were

later attested to: Dacia Repensis along the bank of the
Danube, with Ritiaria as its capital city, and Dacia Medi-
terranea in the middle of the country, within the Balkan
Peninsula, with Serdica (Sofia) as its capital city.

The theory of the evacuation of the entire population
of the province, which has been advanced by some historians, was not possible or justified by anything that
happened and, indeed, is contradicted by the evidence
of Roman and Daco-Roman remains relating to periods
after the third century unearthed by archaeologists.
Aurelian did not withdraw from Dacia forced by special
events which could have fallen upon the province. There
is no written source stating that there was "a complete
evacuation of the Dacian population". Eutropius and
Rufius Festus specify that the Romans were withdrawn
from Dacia. In *Historia Augusta* they say that Aurelian
withdrew the army and "the provincials". The people
Aurelian brought out from Dacia were placed in Moesia.
According to Jordanes, the Empire transferred only the
legions south of the Danube.

A more critical and careful analysis of the sources
quoted emphasizes the fact, firmly underlined by the
most famous Romanian and foreign historians, that it
was the army, the administration and the rich Roman
stratum that was transferred south of the Danube. The
largest part of the Daco-Roman population therefore
remained. This historical reality has been fully confirmed
by the archaeological discoveries and by the study of
inscriptions and coins. On the territory of the former
province (Transylvania, Banat and Oltenia), researchers
have discovered numerous traces of the post-Aurelian
material culture, which provides conclusive proof of the
persistence of the Daco-Roman population in the countryside, as well as in the urban and military centres. As
revealed by these discoveries, this was a dense population
spread over the entire territory of the former province,
able to face the migratory invasions of the following
centuries. No demographical changes or changes in the
material culture have been found in the areas reorganized administratively by the Romans south of the
Danube. No source mentions, after the date of the withdrawal, a Dacian ethnic presence south of the Danube
in spite of the creation there in memory of the abandoned province, of two administrative units, the Dacia
Ripensis and Dacia Mediterranea.

The nature of the withdrawal, as the events that followed it make clear, proves not only the presence of a massive Daco-Roman population in the north part of the Danube but also the care the Empire took of those left in the former province. In order to maintain a permanent link with them, the Romans kept a few important bridgeheads on the left side of the Danube, at Sucidava, Desa, Bistreţu, Drobeta, Dierna, Gornea etc. During Constantine the Great's reign (306-37), the Romans consolidated their position in the north of the Danube, extending their domination of all the Danube Plain to "Novac's Furrow", an imaginary line, based on legend, between Turnu Severin and Buzău. The Empire also built a new bridge over the Danube at Celei-Sucidava and the fortresses Turris and Constantiana Daphne.

Aurelian's withdrawal, entailing the elimination of the boundaries of Dacia province, achieved again the territorial unity of all the Dacians and the Daco-Romans. Now the free Dacians from the west as well as some groups of free Dacians from east of the Carpathians could move to the centre of Transylvania, a fact proved by the archaeological discoveries at Cîpau-Gîrle (Mureş district) and Sopteriu (Bistriţa-Năsăud district).

It is well known that after the withdrawal of the Romans from the province of Dacia a migration of the Germanic populations of the Goths and the Taifals took place in the east. Though the boundaries of the province no longer existed, these migrants settled on the territory of the free Dacians east and south of the Carpathians without penetrating the former Roman Dacia. Only later, in the second half of the fourth century AD, some Germanic groups arrived in Transylvania. This situation is another argument for the belief that the remaining Daco-Roman population in the province was not only numerous but also well organized so that they did not allow the first migratory populations to enter their territories. It is almost certain that in this respect the Romans played an important role because, concluding agreements with the Goths, they introduced among the clauses one forbidding them to enter and to settle on the former territories of Roman Dacia. Taking into consideration this last fact, added to those given above, the claim may be made that only the Roman army and administration, plus the wealthier citizens, withdrew from Dacia, the Daco-Roman population and many colonists remaining on this territory, where they continued to live and further develop.

Now that the historical background has been outlined, I will add at some length information about Dacian settlements and fortresses as revealed by archaeological research.

4. Dacian Fortresses and Settlements (6th Century BC—2 nd Century AD)

The work of Romania's archaeologists has not only brought to light features such as fortresses, parts of buildings, fire pits, kilns, storage pits, ceramics, coins and objects used in the household, in farming and in hunting and war, but has also helped to identify places named in ancient chronicles but since then allowed to slip out of sight.

It is unanimously agreed today that the word *dava* was used by the Geto-Dacians to denote what other people called *oppidum* or *polis,* in other words, a city seat, the centre of a political unit. What we know so far shows us that the settlements in the territory inhabited by the Geto-Dacians can be grouped into open settlements, fortified settlements (some of which were of the *dava* type) and strongholds. Special attention was given to the Geto-Dacian *davae* by Ptolemy, whose *Geography* records over forty *poleis* in Dacia. Archaeological excavations, especially in the last two decades, have brought to light a considerable number of *davae,* some of which were also hypothetically identified.

A very large labour force would have been necessary to build some of the fortifications. Discussing Dacia prior to the Roman conquest in her book *Continuity of the Romanian People's Material and Spiritual Production in the Territory of Former Dacia,* the archaeologist Ligia Bârzu said that, despite the lack of written information, we still can admit that the king and the local aristocracy had the right of coercion over the lower classes:

"Among the most burdensome duties must have been the *corvées* (duty labour or forced labour), and we have no reason to doubt that they were exacted ; the evidence is in the fortifications, beginning with the simple moat and *vallum* (rampart) and ending with the complex fortifications including a precinct wall, towers, tanks etc.

Even if we admitted that Greek masters were hired to make such defensive buildings like the ones we can see in the Orăştie Mountains, a fact confirmed by the Greek letters carved in stone, the enormous amount of work required by such an undertaking could only have been contributed by the locals.

"The terraces and suspended balconies (at Piatra Craivii, for example), the cutting and transportation of stone blocks, tree felling and transport, the arrangement of the drums and the temple columns, the digging of the moats and the building of palisades — everything bespeaks of a tremendous amount of work and perfect co-ordination of operations. The free members of the community could only be asked to contribute unpaid labour to undertakings of communal interest, as for instance to build the refuge strongholds or sanctuaries."

The research done until now has proved that in most cases the Geto-Dacian settlements were placed in naturally sheltered areas. Fortified settlements standing on protruding terraces, isolated promontories or at the top of hills surrounded by steep slopes difficult of access are characteristic. To increase security, the Geto-Dacians expanded and completed the defensive system with manmade work in those parts that were vulnerable. Fortified settlements were known from the beginning of the Geto-Dacian civilization, the earliest being the stronghold at Stînceşti, Botoşani county, which is dated to the sixth century BC. The fortified complex there, made of two adjoining earthen strongholds, covered nearly fifty hectares. Its existence was brought to a halt in the third century BC. Smaller in area, but in many ways similar to the one at Stînceşti, are the fortified settlements at Copălău-Poiana, Costăchel and Victoria-Stăuceni (Botoşani county). We may add to these the important settlements at Cotnari and Moşna (Jassy county), Arsura (Vaslui county), Brăhă-şeşti (Galaţi county) and Albeşti, Zimnicea and Orbeasca de Sus (Teleorman county). Highly interesting also are the settlements at Mărgăriteşti and Morunglav (Olt county), Bucovăţ and Coţofenii din Dos (Dolj county) and Bestepe-Mahmudia commune (Tulcea county). These are dated to the fourth to second centuries BC and for the most part are fortified centres showing only slight evidence of habitation, having been used mainly as places of refuge.

Archaeological research has shown that, in fortifying their settlements, the Geto-Dacians used simple defensive elements, such as moats, *valla*, palisades and more complex fortifications consisting of moat and palisade, *vallum* and palisade, moat and *vallum*. In some places stone walls were built with clay as a binder.

The various types of Geto-Dacian settlements and fortifications allow us to draw some general conclusions on the character and functions of the major classes of fortified settlements in Dacia.

A first category could be identified as a place conceived not as a settlement proper but rather as a fortified place of refuge. Standing on high terraces, surrounded by moats and *valla*, these places enclosed unusually large areas ranging from a couple of hectares (Morunglav, Cotnari, Moşna) to twenty to twenty-five hectares (Mărgăriteşti, Arsura, Beştepe) and even fifty hectares (Stînceşti, Bucovăţ). These places do not show signs of actual habitation. Most of these fortresses which were not places of habitation date from the early Geto-Dacian civilization, spanning the sixth to third centuries BC.

A second large category of fortified places includes the settlements proper, the *davae* more particularly. These are defined as centres of tribes and especially unions of tribes founded to meet military and political needs and to fulfil several functions. In this connection we may draw attention to the main type of *davae* such as those at Popeşti, Crăsani, Cîrlomăneşti, Poiana, Răcătău, Brad, Sprîncenata, Ocniţa, Pecica etc, which have been shown to be primarily political centres, the seat of the leadership of the tribe or union of tribes. As the wealth and variety of finds show, these settlements were all major residential centres. No doubt they also provided shelter at times of danger to the population living in the unfortified settlements in the neighbourhood.

We should also take into account the significant economic role played by these settlements of the Geto-Dacian society at the time of its highest development in the second century BC to the first century AD. A number of finds made to date indicate that *davae* were major economic centres, seats where goods were manufactured and trade took place. The proof of this is supplied not only by the metal workshops at Popeşti on the Argeş, the iron-ore reducing kilns at Brad and the ones used to fire vessels at Deva and Poiana but also by the artefacts used to make a certain class of object, alongside unfinished items and rejects, metal cakes and slag, as well as considerable quantities of highly diverse archaeological finds (pottery, objects of decoration, coins etc.). The *dava* at Popeşti shows that it once contained pottery workshops which made goods of a high technical and artistic level as well as the common types of vessel in the local tradition, imitations of Delian and Megarian bowls with relief decorations as well as amphorae. The moulds of stemware with relief decoration unearthed at Crăsani, Poiana and Popeşti and the bowls or fragments of them found in over thirty-five places indicate the development and diversification of the Geto-Dacian pottery. At Pecica, where various types of vessels were made in large quantities, a jeweller's workshop was found. Dacian objects of decoration of silver, bronze and iron were made there; it is thought that gold was reserved for the use of the king. A minting and jewel-making workshop seems to have functioned at the important Getic centre of Poiana (Galaţi county). A handicraft shop was uncovered at Ardeu (Hunedoara county), as was a workshop dwelling at Tăşad (Bihor county). Even if direct evidence is still lacking, it may be assumed that similar handicraft and minting workshops existed in the other Geto-Dacian *davae* as well, if we bear in mind that at that time the Geto-Dacians had issued many coins and were making a considerable quantity of silver objects of decoration and vessels.

In all the *davae* investigated so far, without exception, many Greek and Roman imports have been found, among which were ceramics, coins and objects of personal decoration. These finds can give us a fair idea of who the Geto-Dacians traded with and the nature and volume of their trade. The major Geto-Dacian *davae* in the three centuries that preceded the Roman conquest were also religious centres. On the whole, the variety of finds in the *davae* supply ample evidence of their mixed character, their economic, political and military function intertwining with the religious one.

It is not surprising that "*dava*" is incorporated in many place-names (Ziridava, Sucidava, Piroboridava etc). Though not specifically showing what a *dava* was, ancient sources make numerous references to these city-seats. For instance, Arrian tells us that in 335 BC, in his expedition north of the Danube, Alexander the Great fought against the Getae grouped around a stronghold not far from the river bank. Archaeological investigations conducted at Zimnicea have shown that a *dava* developed there from the fourth to the first century BC. It is not known if this was the stronghold Alexander the Great came upon in his campaign north of the Danube. Chronologically, it is one of the first strongholds recorded in history.

The Bucharest Institute of Archaeology and the Rîmnicu Vîlcea County Museum have for fifteen years been conducting systematic and wide-ranging archaeological excavations at Ocniţa in Oltenia. A rich archaeological and historical documentation has been assembled each year during these excavations, enabling a clear-cut image of the history of the Geto-Dacian community of the Vîlcea sub-Carpathians and the north-western part of Wallachia to emerge. A complex of settlements, fortified heights and a cemetery were discovered at a point known as Cosota-Ocniţa. Three heights, at approximately five hundred metres above sea-level, were fortified with defensive *valla* surmounted by palisades on three sides. At some points watch and defence towers had been erected.

The clay vessels worked on the wheel found at Ocniţa have elegant shapes, some of them being attractively ornamented either with glazed stripes disposed in a geometric pattern characteristic of Thracian art or with painted decorative motifs of unusual beauty and originality. The vast majority of the vessels were of ancient local tradition whereas others were made after Roman and Greek models. The discoveries made at Ocniţa have added considerably to the archaeological-historical documentation of how the Geto-Dacians assimilated the elements of advanced civilizations and transformed them according to their tastes and needs. At the time of Burebista the use of the potter's wheel went hand in hand with the traditional hand-modelling of the vessels.

In the course of their excavations the archaeologists found in many places traces of iron-ore reduction, tools in the process of being finished, vessels in which the metal for small and delicate objects was melted and cast, and pieces of slag, all of them pointing to iron metallurgy as having been a systematic pursuit of the local population. Tools used in the exploitation of salt, farming, fishing and hunting were also discovered. Many weapons were also excavated, from sling stones, arrow tips and sabres with curved blades (the famous Dacian sabres) to Roman spades (or broad swords). Such a "spade" was uncovered in 1973 in an underground chamber. It was in its scabbard, which showed unmistakable signs of surface burns obviously caused by a fire which destroyed the whole of the fortified complex on the Ocniţa heights investigated so far.

Signs of a huge fire were also found in the civil settlement lying at the foot of the slope. This fire has been connected by historians with a historic and military event and can be explained by a sweeping campaign started by the Romans in the Danube area and continued as far as the Vîlcea and Argeş sub-Carpathians. The same chamber in which the Roman "spade" was discovered contained two coins also showing signs of burns, minted under the reign of Augustus, the end of the first century BC or possibly the beginning of the next century.

It is known that the Roman state had extended its rule as far as the Danube and that the Roman armies' excursions often took them north of the river. One such excursion was carried out in the reign of Augustus and was led by Sextus Aelius Catus who, according to written sources, moved some fifty thousand Getae south of the Danube into the Roman Empire. This was a large-scale expedition which caused, during the years AD 9-11, the fire already referred to. The part played by other Geto-Dacian fortresses standing between the Danube and the Carpathians, such as those at Zimnicea, Popeşti and Crăsani, ceased about the same time. From then onwards, the Dacian military centres of the Romanian plain and the southern Carpathians ceased to play the part of defence fortresses against the Romans but life continued to develop in their vicinity, although the population seems to have become rather sparse in certain areas, probably due to the displacements enforced by the Romans.

One of the discoveries that has aroused particular interest among scientists in Romania and abroad refers to the oldest evidence of writing with Latin characters known so far in the territories inhabited by the Getae and the Dacians, who, as generally admitted, were one people, speaking one language, Thracian. During excavations conducted in 1973 and 1978, fragments of pottery at Ocniţa were uncovered which showed grazed names with Latin letters. A fragment of a vase carried the inscription BUR, indicating the name of the tribe or union of tribes, the Buridavensi Dacians who lived at Buridava and who were mentioned by Ptolemy in the second century AD under the name of Buridavensioi as a tribe of Dacia. This discovery is also of historic significance in that we have at present, thanks to the inscriptions already mentioned, the only source of the time on which we can locate, with great precision, a *dava* that is at least one Dacian fortress of the forty-four recorded by Ptolemy. We know too that it was at Ocniţa that the important economic and military centre of Buridava was once located. In addition to the inscriptions in Latin capitals and cursives uncovered in 1973 and 1978, two inscriptions in Greek were discovered in the same years. They both date from the time of Augustus and contain information of exceptional value. One of them carries the word *Basileus (Basilcos* in Greek), meaning head or king, and seems to have been written before the vessel was hardened by fire. Both inscriptions contain the name of the king which was completed by experts in the form of Thiemarcus. The list of Dacian kings who succeeded Burebista and preceded Decebalus is thus completed with the addition of one more king who was not known before 1973.

This fact has yet another significance. The Greek historian Strabo who, in his youth, was one of Burebista's contemporaries and who had more knowledge about more events than any other other writer of antiquity, tells us that following the "overthrow" of Burebista by a handful of rebels, the Dacian state was dismembered, first into four and later into five separate kingdoms. One of these kingdoms was ruled by Deceneu, the high priest and Burebista's closest adviser, who according to Jordanes, the Gothic historian (mid-sixth century AD) held "almost royal" powers. This small Dacian kingdom may have been situated in the intra-Carpathian area and may have had Buridava as its capital. The other four kingdoms cannot be located. What we do know for certain is that the Dacian Buridava (or Ocniţa as it is known today) was the capital of a micro-state ruled by King Thiemarcus. This demonstrates that after the death of Burebista the state tradition was perpetuated south of the Carpathians.

In historical research, Petrodava, another *dava* named by Ptolemy, is an example of the need for complex investigations before its location could be established. To this end, research had to be done in geography, linguistics and archaeology. In his *Geography,* Ptolemy places Petrodava at $53°45'$ longitude and $47°40'$ latitude. With this information as a basis, it had long been assumed that Petrodava would have been somewhere in the west or north-west of Moldova (Moldavia). Given the relativity of Ptolemy's co-ordinates and in order to locate the *dava* more accurately, comparison was made with the other three *davae* which the Greek geographer recorded on the Siret (Poroboridava, Tamasidava and Zargidava), which recent field investigations have identified as the *davae* at Poiana (Galați county), Răcătău and Brad (Bacău county). On the basis of this additional information the researchers concluded that Petrodava should be sought in the sub-Carpathian area, with investigations concentrating on Piatra Neamț and Piatra Soimului which are twenty kilometres apart, since in both places interesting Geto-Dacian vestiges had been found.

Now it was the turn of linguistics to make its contribution : could the root *Petro* not have in the Geto-Dacian language the same significance as *petra* had in both Latin and Greek, i.e. rock, stone ? The meaning of the modern toponym Piatra Neamț (with Mount Pietricica towering over the city) added weight to this argument. Significantly, the name of the place has emphasized throughout its existence the relief detail. In the Middle Ages it was called Piatra lui Craciun ; now its name is Piatra Neamț. As the people who live there today just call it Piatra, it was only natural to assume that the ancients called it Petrodava.

The geographical and philological arguments were strengthened by the numerous evidences of Geto-Dacian settlements in the Piatra Neamț area, the most spectacular of which are the stone fortifications and sanctuaries on Bîtca Doamnei, a rocky hill three or four kilometres west of the city. At the foot of the hill, where the Bistrița river bed used to be, there is today a storage lake. The eastern and northern slopes of the hill are very steep, and as the western one is far more gentle, the Geto-Dacians built their homes there on three successive terraces. The connection with the nearby mountain was through a narrow saddle where the ancient road also wound to the gate of the stronghold, which was enclosed by a stone wall about 3.5 metres thick. The entrance to the stronghold was through a tower with a square base (nine metres by nine metres) and with an upper part made of clay and beams ; in ancient times it would have been at least seven metres high. The stone for the building, which would have been found locally, was roughly cut. The rocky blocks were laid in two rows between which was a filling of chipped stone. A clay binder was used by the builders to give the structure the necessary strength. Archaeological finds old wooden poles showing indications of a fire implied to the researchers that the wall used to have an upper part made of wood. The height of the wall cannot be estimated accurately today ; it is supposed to have been four or five metres at the most.

Inside the stronghold several dwellings were identified, all of rectangular shape, with stone foundations, walls made of beams and a shingle-covered roof. A larger dwelling, probably with several rooms, on the upper part of the plateau on which the stronghold stood, may have been the home of the local chieftain.

But by far the most remarkable find at Bîtca Doamnei were the traces of two sanctuaries whose plan and stone-drum rows were analogous to those of the Dacian sanctuaries identified in the Orăştie Mountains.

The excavations undertaken over several years at the place which the ancients called Petrodava brought to light the usual inventory of the Geto-Dacian settlements: local and imported ceramics (Greek and Roman), iron implements, objects of decoration, stone mills etc. A frequent find was the fine brown wheel-worked pottery decorated with red strips or geometric designs to be found chiefly in Moldova. Imported objects were relatively scarce. Among a few items worth notice, mainly fragments of amphorae, was a gilded bronze vessel with a handle shaped like a human head at its lower part.

The collection of objects with the few coins unearthed at Bîtca Doamnei made the researchers assume that the settlement was founded in the second century BC and that it began to flourish in the following century. The stone fortifications and at least one of the sanctuaries were datable to that flourishing period. A huge fire put an end to the settlement and to the first phase of the stronghold as well. It is not possible to say when this event occurred. There is no reason to believe that the stronghold at Petrodava could have escaped the fate that befell the three other Geto-Dacian *davae* on the Siret which were subject to great damage in the wake of the events that took place between AD 89 (the year when Decebalus made peace with Domitian) and 106 (the end of the war with the Romans). There is not yet enough archaeological evidence to provide an answer to such questions that involve events occurring over a certain period.

As the research conducted so far shows, the stronghold at Bîtca Doamnei (Petrodava) was rather similar to an acropolis, being the political and religious centre of the Geto-Dacians in the Neamţ area. The everyday life of the people was going on in open settlements in the area around the dava.

Another fortification was identified on Mount Cozia: largely destroyed by modern works, it allowed only a cursory investigation. However, the finds show that it was contemporary with the fortifications on Bîtca Doamnei. Why should two strongholds have been thought necessary within only four kilometres? No satisfactory answer can be given at present. All one can say is that the concentration of numerous Geto-Dacian ruins and objects in so small an area points to the significance of this political and economic centre. Also, the analogies of the stronghold at Bîtca Doamnei with the Dacian monuments in the Orăştie Mountains supply yet another indisputable proof of the unity of material and spiritual culture of the Geto-Dacians when their development was at its peak.

The identification cf Tamasidava, another *dava* in the Siret valley, also posed problems for the researchers. A first attempt was made by the Austrian historian and geographer Wilhelm Tomascheck, who set it in the Bîrlad area in his work on *Old Thracians*. Vasile Pârvan placed the same *dava* near Bacău, whereas Vasile Cihodaru located it at Stoeneşti, Vaslui county. Finally, in the wake of the excavations in the Geto-Dacian settlement at Brad-Negri, Bacău county, in 1963, Aleandru Vulpe and Vasile Ursachi were convinced that they had located Tamasidava.

The research undertaken after 1968 by the Bacău Museum of History jointly with that of the town of Roman resulted in the uncovering at Răcătău, in the middle course of the Siret, of an *oppidum* identified as Tamasidava. The fortified settlement was on a 170 metre high terrace near the Siret, a highly favourable location. The highest place on the western ridge of the Tutova Hills, surrounded by steep valleys, it was well protected. In fact, only the political and military settlement — the acropolis — suggestively called by the local inhabitants *Cetăţuia* (the fortress) stood high up on the terrace. The toponym has endured to this day. The civil settlement, where dwellings specific of the Daco-Getae in the first century BC to first century AD were identified, was in the vicinity of the acropolis. Within one kilometre a cemetery was found. With the valleys around forming a natural defensive system, the acropolis was, as a result of human labour, virtually impregnable. On the side overlooking the civil settlement, the Geto-Dacians had dug a deep moat and a palisade.

The *dava* at Răcătău, as Tamasidava is now called, witnessed, in the main, peaceful events, being, in the favourable conditions provided by the Siret valley, a main trading centre and a meeting-place for the Geto-Dacian population all over Moldova and foreign merchants, Greeks and eventually Romans, who had settled on the western and southern shores of the Black Sea. The rich collection of tools, ceramics, objects of personal decoration, cult items and fibulae (brooches or clasps) found there adds to our knowledge of how busy trade was in the Geto-Dacian community. Imported ceramics in large quantities and variously shaped, with many items showing a higher technique than was available locally (amphorae, marmites [earthenware cooking vessels], two-handled vessels of the *kantharos* type), point to Tamasidava as being a true market centre where foreign merchants came with their wares which eventually reached the smaller places in the district through local traders who acted as intermediaries.

The very busy trade that went on at Tamasidava is proved by the discovery of three hoards consisting of republican Roman coins dating to 175 BC and imperial ones issued by Augustus, Tiberius, Claudius and Nero, as well as Dacian coins, among which those of the Vîrteju-Bucharest type were the more interesting since they proved the scope of the exchanges with the population of the Romanian plain.

Very large quantities of local pottery were also found, both fine ceramics, worked by wheel in a variety of forms, and handmade, such as the jar-shaped vessel or the rushlight cup (the Dacian cup, used as a lid to cover the urn.). Apart from ceramics, an impressive number of bronze and iron objects were brought to light, among which were coulters, knives, forks, axes, chisels, nails, arrows and spearheads, as well as harness parts. Tamasidava was not only a very important trading centre but also a major manufacturing settlement. The many items of agricultural tools indicate a stable community, with tilling the land playing an important role in its economic life.

Highly interesting were the zoomorphic and anthropomorphic figurines associated with what were probably magic and cult functions. On a *kantharos*-type vessel a zoomorphic and anthropomorphic design can be seen, with a knight carrying a short sword fastened to his belt and probably a flag in his right hand. Each of the handles shows the solar disc flanked by lions. Another vessel of local make has a small plate attached to it showing a local deity, a strange-looking Silenus with the ears of an ass, possibly the protector of farmers and shepherds. Other items show cattle and sheep, and there are vessels whose handles feature the heads of ducks and sheep. A couple of anthropomorphic figurines made of a thick paste were also discovered. Grey or brownish in colour, they show rudimentary figures of men and women.

It is clear from the large number of objects uncovered at Răcătău, and from the variety of them, that Tamasidava, whose development reached a peak in the second century BC to first century AD, was one of the major economic centres of the Geto-Dacians in Moldavia.

The search for Zargidava, another *dava* on the Siret, led to the conclusion that in all probability this was the ancient name of Brad, a town noted for its mines. Of the seventy settlements known to have belonged to the Romanians' forebears, the *dava* at Brad, situated on the left terrace of the Siret on a promontory which ensured it a dominant position with admirable visibility and excellent natural defences, is noteworthy for its size, age and density of habitation.

It is obvious that the history of this settlement, which was one of the most flourishing cities of ancient Dacia, goes far back into the past. The origins of the settlement can be traced back to the neolithic era. Of all the historic epochs, that of the Geto-Dacians was by far the richest and the best authenticated, the time during which they lived in this fortress spanning a period of almost six centuries (fourth century BC to second century AD). Researchers point out that until the time of King Burebista the settlement was rather small, with a fortification which went back to the Bronze Age, but during Burebista's reign the fortifications were considerably reinforced. The defence ditch was widened and deepened and the acropolis enclosed with wooden palisades. In the area of the front gate an ingenious defence construction was erected, consisting of vertically and obliquely arranged sharp-pointed stakes, which made access to the acropolis practically impossible to any would-be attacker.

The investigations conducted here revealed the existence of a large agglomeration of dwellings around an enclosed yard or market-place, an *agora* paved with gravel, which may have been where the inhabitants used to meet to take the more important decisions. This was the first discovery of its kind in the Dacian fortresses. It supplies important information as to the social organization of these fortresses during the final period of military democracy. Excavations carried out in the immediate vicinity of the enclosed yard exposed a large building, one of the best preserved of all the similar buildings that have been discovered in Moldavia. This building, which had several rooms, each with a fireplace in the middle, and interior walls decorated with a variety of drawings, could have been the residence of the ruler.

The other buildings in this fortress were similar to those found several decades ago in this part of Moldavia : one-room dwellings with clay floors, with wattle-and-daub or wooden walls covered with reed, wood tiles or straw. Judging by the 250 fireplaces that have been discovered so far, the number of dwellings may have been large. The 180 or so food pits that have been uncovered lead to the conclusion that the main pursuit of the inhabitants was agriculture. The number of fireplaces superimposed on older ones provided clear evidence of uninterrupted habitation : since the space available within the fortress was rather limited, new houses were often built on the ruins of older ones which had been destroyed by age, fires or by other causes, which accounts for the fact that one hearth could have two, three, or even seven (in one case twelve) superimposed fireplaces built on it, maybe by just as many generations.

Excavations also brought to light iron axes which were used mainly to clear the woods, as well as sickles and ploughshares which, along with the remains of calcinated millet, point to the widespread development of agriculture. Arrow, pike and spear tips, as well as iron stirrups, some of them silver-plated, have also been discovered. The number of such objects is fairly small, which is to be expected, since during the first centuries of its existence life in that area was rather peaceful and later on the conquering Romans captured much of the military equipment of the defeated Dacians.

Most of the inventory of the *dava* at Brad consists of vessels, jars, cups and fruit dishes — hand-made or wheel-worked — after traditional shapes as well as local imitations of Greek models. The abundance of this last-named category and also of painted pottery is yet another proof that a strong trading centre, where pottery was produced for a vast surrounding area, had been in operation at Zargidava. The most valuable pieces discovered here include a large number of beautiful silver, bronze and iron ornaments (bracelets, earrings, kits for needles and pincers, even bone hairpins in the shape of a swan's head, which illustrate the civilized taste which had prompted the production of such objects. Melting-pots, which showed traces of melted iron, iron slag and, most particularly, the bronze bars discovered in this locality, provide the evidence that it was a centre for manufactured goods.

The inhabitants of this large Dacian settlement took an active part in trading exchanges with the population of the neighbouring settlements as well as with the Greek and Roman merchants who came there with their wares. The importance of these trading exchanges is also indicated by the finds in the settlement of many Dacian and Roman (republican and imperial) coins.

Taking into account the fact that no other settlement has been identified north of Răcătău that would deserve the name of *dava* due to its size and importance, all the indications are that Zargidava was the ancient name of Brad.

However, some *davae* still remain to be identified. A fortification system with a *vallum,* marked as an unknown Dacian stronghold, has been uncovered on a promontory in the locality of Buneşti-Avereşti, Vaslui county, in the centre of Moldavia where archaeologist Violeta Bazarciuc of Huşi has excavated objects of decoration, tools and coins. The inventory of objects and coins of particular value for the fourth to second centuries BC includes a large treasure of Geto-Dacian silver ornaments, consisting of fourteen Thracian-type fibulae, fifteen conic and simple-ended rings, bracelets made up of octagonal bars, a multi-spiral bracelet which ended in serpents' heads, and a silver drachm belonging to the last issue of coins by the Greek city of Histria. Later this treasure was completed with ten Dacian silver coins, copies of the tetradrachms of Philip II and Alexander the Great, and two silver bracelets, also made of octagonal bars. In addition, coloured simulated beads, human mask beads, Celtic fibulae, two deposits of tools, ceramics and vessels containing carbonized wheat have also been discovered.

This stronghold obviously played an important part in the trade with the Greek colonies of the Black Sea coast, especially with Histria, whose merchants went to sell their goods as far as the centre of today's Moldavia. Through its location and construction the Buneşti-Avereşti Dacian stronghold held an important place in the Dacian system of defence against the raids of Scythian tribes. Moreover, the rich silver treasure highlights the craftsmanship of the Dacians in working this metal. The results of excavations at this settlement also clarify important questions on the formation of Geto-Dacian civilization in Moldavia, a continuation of the Thracian one, and confirm the ethnic and cultural unity of the population inhabiting the Carpatho-Danubian-Pontic area.

I will return to some of the more interesting discoveries in Moldavia in the next chapter but will now examine the remote area of Oarţa de Sus in Maramureş (northern Transylvania), where the investigations of archaeologist Carol Kacso, of Baia Mare, have brought to light a settlement from the Bronze Age (sixteenth to thirteenth centuries BC) where a most unusual custom of the people who lived then was horse burials, something previously unknown to Romanian archaeologists. This ritual had not been reported before within the Sighişoara-Wietenberg culture to which the settlement belongs.

Alongside a human tomb (in which a treasure consisting of four gold bracelets and one silver bracelet, seventeen gold rings and one silver ring, was found by the Baia Mare archaeologist), was one in which two horses had been laid side by side, bent, with their legs up. On the skeletons were found many vessels, some of them intact and some deliberately broken. On top of these horses lying at the bottom of the tomb another horse had been thrown, over which vessels and small sacrificed animals had also been deposited.

The closest analogies of these horse burials are to be found in the Aegean world (Marathon and Salamis), and their presence in the north of Romania throws new light on the mutual influence between the proto-Thracian communities of the same time.

Archaeological excavations carried out in the Mos-tiştea valley in the Danube plain in recent years have led to the identification of approximately fifty Geto-Dacian settlements. The unusual size and position of some of these settlements classify them as quasi-urban centres inhabited by Dacians. One such settlement of greater importance situated within the radius of Valea Argovei commune (Ilfov district) is named Vlădiceasca. Lying on an island known to the local people as Gher-găul, the settlement has been inhabited ever since neolithic times. The island provides extremely favour-able natural conditions for life with its five-metre high plateau above water-level and with steep slopes difficult to climb. The surrounding slopes make this place even more secure.

Researches conducted so far over an area totalling almost half of the island's size have exposed forty-four dwellings. Bell-shaped storage pits of burnt clay were uncovered in many places in the settlement. One con-struction contains three fortresses of which one had fire-places beautifully decorated with incised lines. Fireplaces decorated in this manner have also brought to light at Popeşti on the Argeş, at Poiana (Galaţi district) and at Cirlomăneşti (Bacău district). They are thought to have been built for religious observances, which means that such a place of worship existed also at Vlădiceasca.

Apart from a large quantity of local and imported pottery, among the discoveries were a fragment of a sil-ver vessel, different silver and bronze ornaments and adornments (plaques, fibulae and bracelets) as well as iron implements and weapons (knives, daggers). To these may be added two salvers of baked clay which may have been used in the sun-worship ritual, judging by their round-discoidal shape.

After rather a quiet period in the beginning, namely about 250-150 BC, the *dava* at Vlădiceasca experienced a time of maximum development in 150-50 BC. After that, the population began to decline, and occupation of the settlement is believed to have come to an end at the beginning of the first century AD, possibly in the wake of the north Danubian expedition undertaken by Aelius Catus in AD 9-12.

The settlement at Vlădiceasca must have been a tribal centre with political, economic, cultural and reli-gious functions. A closer look at the topography of the Mostiştea valley revealed that the larger number of settlements were surrounded by smaller ones. From this point of view, Vlădiceasca represented the classical type, with smaller settlements surrounding it in the area between the present-day villages of Frăsinet and Siliştea. It was on this territory, ruled at that time by a tribal community, that the local people were engaged in agriculture, cattle-raising, hunting and fishing. It is obvious that the *davae*, both large and small, were nuclei of political formations in existence before, during and after Burebista's rule. A less important centre, but similar in many respects to the boroughs of the Middle Ages, the *dava* at Vlădiceasca represented an intermediate stage between the village and the large *davae* such as those at Popeşti, Cîrlomăneşti and others mentioned earlier in the chapter which acted as centres of important tribal unions.

We will now consider the *dava* at Piscul Crăsani (Ialomiţa district). It was described by the Romanian archaeologist Ion Andriescu in 1924 as follows :

Going along the bank of the Ialomiţa terrace, Piscul Crăsani captures the eye as one of its numerous prominences. Advancing more than the others, it must have been a truly formidable natural fortress when intact, judging by its steep slopes. Broken off today by the plain — a former earth *vallum* and fosse — "Piscul" has been turned into three plateaus by continuous landslides. Looking over the water of the Ialomiţa one can see them : one to the west, another in the middle (looking more like a continuous strip of land), the third to the east (long and bending like an arc, embracing the others...). According to researches, the two mounds one large, the other small — guarding "The Peak" approximately one kilometre away from the plain, had no connection whatsoever with the settlement on the bank.

The results of the first investigations started by Dimitrie Butculescu in 1870 enabled Cesar Bolliac to define, for the first time, the characteristics of Dacian material culture. The settlement aroused the interest of scientists following the diggings conducted by Ion Andriescu, and the excavations carried out by Vasile Pârvan, as well as by the Ialomiţa District Museum and the Bucharest Institute of Archaeology after 1969.

Like all other *davae* of the Geto-Dacians, the settlement at Piscul Crăsani was the political, military, economic, cultural and religious centre of a tribal formation. It had an acropolis and, most characteristically, open settlements of different sizes which depended directly on the aristocracy of the fortress. The acropolis was situated on the "Peak", being isolated and naturally defended by deep and almost vertical precipices which went down to the Ialomiţa on the east, north and west sides. To the south, the isolation was ensured by a fairly deep ditch which separated the acropolis from the rest of the terrace, where the most important of the settlements surrounding the fortress was situated. Other open settlements stood at the foot of the peak, to the northeast, another some eight hundred metres to the east and a third further south.

Piscul Crăsani is known to have been inhabited from ancient times. In the neolithic age it was the site where a large settlement belonging to the Boian culture was in existence, strengthened with a defence fosse discovered thirty metres south of the Getic ditch. Other traces of habitation are dated to the first Iron Age. The settlement as such, however, came into being towards the end of the fourth century BC and the beginning of the following century. At first it was a small unfortified settlement but developed gradually, due mostly to the natural resources of the area and to its formidable strategic position. In the second century BC it became the centre of a tribal formation which is believed to have belonged to the federation of Getic tribes which inhabited the central and eastern parts of the Wallachian plain. In the latter half of the second century the settlement was reinforced with a defence ditch and turned into an acropolis for other settlements that had appeared in the surrounding area.

Apart from agriculture and cattle-raising, the trades, dominated by pottery — making and metal-working, flourished. Coarse kitchen pottery has been found along with fine pottery worked on the wheel in traditional shapes or in imitation of Greek models. Worth mentioning are the cups with relief decorations showing original motifs, produced on the spot, which are quite different from the ones discovered in other centres of the Wallachian plain. The adornments and tools found in the area indicate that copper, bronze and silver were the metals in current use at that time.

Piscul Crăsani was also a busy trading centre, not only with the neighbouring Geto-Dacian people but also with the south Danubian, Thracian and Greco-Roman worlds. This view is supported by finds of local or south-Danubian Getic coins and by coins which came from Thasos, Macedonia Prima, Dyrrhachium, Tomis, and the Roman Empire, as well as by imported products such as amphorae from Thasos, Sinope and Rhodes, and Greek figurines.

Life in this *dava* came to an end in the first century BC when open settlements and the necropolis were destroyed by a huge fire, in the wake of which no traces of habitation can be found. Whatever its ancient name (Helis, according to Vasile Pârvan, Netindava, in the opinion of Radu Vulpe), the *dava* at Crăsani was, over the third to first centuries BC, one of the most thriving Geto-Dacian settlements in Wallachia, with a prominent political status and a prosperous economic life until the reign of Burebista.

Archaeological investigations carried out since the middle of the last century at Cetățeni (Argeș district), not far from Cîmpulung-Muscel, have confirmed the presence of an important Geto-Dacian settlement with very good natural defences situated on a high cliff known as Pleașa Popii overlooking the whole valley of the Dîmbovița river.

In contrast with other *davae* of the Romanian plain (Zimnicea, Albești, Popești etc), the settlement at Cetățeni was not fortified. The reason for this is that, unlike the settlements situated in the open fields which required defence walls, that at Cetățeni was protected by the very configuration of the terrain. It is surprising that, despite the absence of walls, the idea of fortress has been perpetuated by the name of the place — Cetățeni — which is one more proof that it has been preserved in the consciousness of generations as a fortified place, even though its "fortification" was a gift of nature.

The *dava* at Cetățeni shows many similarities to the settlement at Popești, looking, in many respects, like a replica of it. Here, too, we are in the presence of a vast construction with one of its walls in the shape of an apse. This seems to have been related to religious observances. Former archaeological reports, drawn up by earlier researchers, also refer to dwellings with stone foundations (which are no longer in existence) but give no details as to the shape and size of these buildings.

The local pottery is of great interest. Excavations exposed large quantities of hand-made vessels, cups of Dacian type and vessels with narrowing bases and bulging bellies (in the shape of two truncated cones). This last-named category also includes a very strange vessel in the shape of a muzzle (*proteoma*) which is similar to a type of Greek vessel (*rhytons*). The wheel-worked pottery includes, for the most part, imitations of cups with decorations in relief, similar to those produced on the isle of Delos, as well as fragments of amphorae with stamps without letters, ornamented with geometric patterns. Both types evince striking similarities to the pottery discovered in the *dava* at Popești, a clear pointer to the existence of close ties between these settlements as well as with the Greek civilization.

The discoveries made at Cetățeni also include iron implements which show that they were made within the fortress itself. They look very similar to the implements found at Popești and Sarmizegetusa.

Important aspects of material life in those parts were revealed by finds of coins. The Romanian historian C. Aricescu reported, as early as 1850, the presence of a Dacian coin of the Vîrteju-Bucharest type which was in circulation at the end of the second century BC as well as coins issued by the west Pontic city of Odessos. The same historian spoke of an amphora which was thought to have contained Roman republican denarii. This assertion could not be checked because the treasure disappeared under circumstances which have not yet been elucidated.

A treasure including two silver fibulae, 121 Roman republican denarii and six coins dating from the time of the Emperor Augustus was discovered at Cetățeni in 1960. One of the coins is of particular interest. It was a denarius issued in 52-50 BC, during the magistrature of C. Cassius Loginus, which shows a Latin inscription made up of four capital letters, PETR, believed to have been scratched on the coin after it was minted, most likely in Dacia, possibly even by the owner of the treasure. The significance of this discovery lies in the fact that it is one of the first indications that writing with Latin letters had been known and used on this territory more than one century before the Roman conquest. This is convincing evidence of the age of the economic and cultural relations between the two worlds and civilizations.

The fortress falls within the same time limits as the *davae* of the Wallachian plain, namely the end of the third century BC to the beginning of the first century AD. We do not know for certain whether the settlement ceased to exist as the result of the expedition of Aelius Catus in AD 9-12 when life in a large number of field *davae* is known to have come to an end. It is very likely that that the northern position of the fortress kept it out of the way of the Roman incursion. If this was so, the life of the fortress may have continued even after that date, though not as a flourishing *dava* as in the past but as a small settlement. The period of the settlement's maximum development coincided with the last decades of the second century BC and the first century BC, reaching its climax during the reign of Burebista.

In the second century BC the Bran Pass played a most significant part as a trading route between the Wallachian plain and Transylvania. The *dava* at Cetăţeni must have had an important role in the economic and political relations of the Geto-Dacian world due to its geographic position. Lying at the gate of the Dîmboviţa defile, before the reaches of the Bran Pass, the role of the *dava* was to direct the whole of the commercial traffic from the Danube plain towards Transylvania and the other way round. The *dava* at Cetăţeni represented, therefore, a first-rank trading centre, ensuring the link between all the Geto-Dacian settlements of the Argeş basin and those in the intra-Carpathian space. By the part it played as a link between these two zones of Dacia, the settlement at Cetăţeni ranks among those which had contributed a great deal to the diffusion, generalization and, in the last analysis, unity of the Geto-Dacian culture and language in general.

A rather later *dava* is that at Filiaşi (Harghita district). Situated on the bank of a riverlet which joins the Tîrnava Mare, the settlement was founded by the free Dacians and is dated to the period following the conquest of Dacia by the Romans. Excavations carried out here have exposed a wide variety of pottery (a fragment of *terra sigillata*, fine Roman pottery decorated with impressed rosettes) and Dacian (wheel-worked vessels of grey paste and fruit dishes, common to the free Dacians of Moldavia as the prevailing type). These indicate the existence of a handicraft and trading centre which supplied the adjoining area as well.

The settlements situated in south-eastern Transylvania show, by their large numbers and abundant archaeological material, that here was a rich local civilization to which was added the influence of other cultures of the time, namely Greek, Roman and Celtic, which did not cause the Geto-Dacian characteristic elements to get lost. This cultural heritage did not disappear after the conquest of part of Dacia but was preserved and handed down along the centuries to the population which remained in these parts after the withdrawal of the Roman legions and administration.

The treasures discovered at Surcea, Ghelinţa and Peteni (all in Covasna district) and at Sincrăieni (Harghita district) round off the economic and social picture of the area, emphasizing the important part played by this region in the processing of precious metals, especially silver. The hoard of coins recently discovered at Hilib (Covasna district), which includes 79 drachmas issued in the city of Dyrrachium, 21 tetradrachmas from Thasos, and a Roman republican denarius dating from 87 BC, provides proof of the close ties maintained by the Dacians living in these parts with the city of Dyrrachium, a famous centre on the coast of the Adriatic. The treasure, which is dated to the beginning of the rule of Burebista, also bears witness to the fact that this area was crossed by a very busy trading route which was an important connection with the Geto-Dacians living on the other side of the Carpathians.

Tibiscum, a settlement on the banks of the River Timis (its ancient name was Tibiscus), was the most outstanding urban centre in the south-west of Roman Dacia. It was elevated to the rank of a *municipium* in the third century. The research conducted recently by archaeologists from Timişoara and Caransebeş led by Dr Doina Benea has unearthed objects of great value for the military history and for the economic and spiritual life of the Daco-Romans. Potteries, smithies, bronzesmiths' and goldsmiths' workshops, stonecutters and other workshops have been found.

A large workshop for the manufacture of glass beads discovered here, with the tools, allows us to reconstitute the various methods of jewel making and the great art of the Daco-Roman craftsmen. The melting installation is identical in construction with one discovered in Switzerland but technically superior to it.

According to these finds, Tibiscum appears to have been one of the major centres of the Roman world in the manufacture of jewels, especially glass beads and semi-precious stones. Roman life at Tibiscum as reconstituted by archaeologists proves that Roman Dacia was a supplier not only of farm produce to the Empire but also of manufactured goods, including luxury objects. The products were also sold to the free Dacians in the north and north-east, and to the Sarmatians. The activity of the locality, which flourished in the third and fourth centuries, ceased on the invasion of the Huns in the late fourth century, when the inhabitants retreated to safer places.

So far we have been considering, in the main, Geto-Dacian settlements and fortifications. We should also bear in mind those erected by the Romans. In *Continuity of the Romanian People's Material and Spiritual Production in the Territory of Former Dacia*, Ligia Bârzu points out that the idea was never accepted by the Empire that Dacia was a territory lost for good and all. A return was at any time possible, and that did not seem to differ from other similar concessions that the Romans had been forced to make at the Rhenish border or on the Euphrates. The fact was that Aurelian himself did not give up the idea of controlling both banks of the Danube. It was highly probable, she considered, that he even undertook to build some special fortifications as the investigations at Sucidava suggest. It seemed that Aurelian must be credited with the early work on the stronghold there.

With the establishment of the dominate and Constantine the Great's rise, Roman authority was spectacularly being restored over the north Danubian space. Not only was the area between the Danube and the sub-Carpathian hilly region in former Dacia Malvensis reintegrated into the Empire, but the boundary of the territory actually administered was pushed further eastward. A complex system of fortifications was being built, including *castra*, castella and towers all along the lower course of the Danube from Gornea (Caraş-Severin) and Drobeta to Dinogetia and Barboşi. The northern boundary of that territory was also strengthened by a *vallum* across the whole Romanian plain, where *castra* were

also erected (Hinova, Pietroasele). The importance
and endurance of that defensive system is proved
by the archaeological complex at Pietroasele (Buzău),
including a *castrum*, *thermae* and several necropo-
lises definitely dating from Constantine until Valens's time . . . . .

In the next chapter we consider the significance of
other discoveries in Moldavia, including relics of ancient
fishermen and hunters.

5. More Discoveries in Moldavia

A solid gold diadem weighing over 750 grams, now in the national collection in the Museum of National History in Bucharest, is among the valuable archaeological finds of the 1984 archaeological year. The diadem, which belonged to an era about two hundred years earlier than the reign of King Burebista, which ended in 44 BC, was found in a dwelling of the Geto-Dacian citadel situated on a hill south of the village of Buneşti, Vaslui county, in the central Moldavian plateau site of great importance for Romanian archaeology. It is part of a series of Geto-Dacian fortifications in Moldavia built in the second half of the fourth century BC probably against the frequent raids by Scythian tribes. On the south side of the citadel there was a defence mound about nine metres high which has been eroded by landslides.

The diadem was found just under half a metre below the surface on a neolithic platform. All the research carried out in the area by excavating a six-metre by twenty-seven-metre surface indicated that the diadem had been taken from a larger hoard and hidden there. The twenty-four-carat gold diadem with a 14.6 to 15.3 centimetre diameter wrought in gold wire of six millimetres diameter was made up of two parallel gold bars joined in six points, creating a few loops to which the gold plate was fixed. The plate features five floral motifs executed in relief, with a gold-plated cylinder in the interior by which the main motif of a flower was supported. The flowers were devised as three six-petal rosettes, bordered by filigree wire. On top there was a six-petal flower with a gold drop in the middle. The ends of the two bars were modelled as stylized animals of prey, with a circular fastening link attached to the mouth of the animal. The empty spaces on the gold bar which separate the body of the animals from their legs had been filled in with a bluish viscous paste which has been preserved only at one end. The name of the prince to whom the diadem belonged is not known. The diadem is an exceptional discovery for that period in the Carpathian-Danube-Pontic territory. There are some similarities only in the manner of representation of the floral patterns with the filigree button which ornamented one of the ends of the necklace belonging to the Băiceni-Cucuteni hoard (Jassy county), dating back to the fourth and third centuries BC.

During seven archaeological research campaigns (1978-84) 46 Geto-Dacian dwellings were discovered in the citadel, all of them of a rectangular shape with slightly rounded corners and a hearth situated north-east or north-west. The inventory was rich : ceramics, iron implements and weapons, gold, silver, bronze, and glass ornaments, coins and ceramics of Greek import. Hand-turned items of ceramics were also found at Buneşti : big double *frustum*-shaped vessels, bell-shaped pots, cups with slightly elevated handles, lids etc. They were decorated with an alveolate band, interrupted by conic prominences, omega-letter or comma-like ornaments in relief and bands of comb-traced undulating lines. By and large, the range of ceramic shapes discovered at Buneşti is analogous with finds throughout the Carpathian-Danubian-Pontic territory, i.e. Zimnicea, Enisala, Poiana, Corni-Huşi, Murighiol. In addition, a few wheel-turned vases have been discovered as well as whole amphorae and vessel shards coming from the Greek world of Thasos, Heraclea, Pontica, Sinope, Cos and Rhodes.

Iron implements were found in storehouses and in the dwellings. In 1980 the first axes found included those with transversal slots, open-socket axes and an axe with small "wings"; drive-pin punches and a plough-share were also discovered. Nothing like these axes has been found in any other settlement of the time. In the first storehouse five Geto-Dacian silver coins which probably date back to the fourth to second centuries BC were found.

In the dwellings other axes were discovered of the same type as those in the storehouses, as well as sickles and wood or bone-handle knives, some pieces still preserving the pins holding the handle. In 1982 a group of tools was discovered in one of the dwellings, tied with two circular iron pieces each provided with a pin. Of the nine axes, five had a transversal slot, three were open-socket and one was of a closed-socket type. From the very first year of research on the Geto-Dacian citadel of Buneşti, iron dross and tools were excavated which proved the existence of workshops for iron processing, a fact confirmed in the following years by the discovery of *frustum*-shaped drive-pin punches, a punch, a pair of compasses and two pairs of forge tongs. It is known that such pieces had been common at the height of Geto-Dacian civilization, the epoch of the great kings Burebista (70-44 BC) and Decebalus (AD 86-106), and their presence in the Buneşti site points to the high level reached in metal processing, this iron civilization being in no way inferior to that in the other known parts of the world of the time. In previous years iron weapons had also been found there : spearbutts and four spearheads with rhomboidal-section blades and a long shaft. A single similar piece was unearthed in the Botosana settlement (Suceava county, also in Moldavia) dating back to the third to second centuries BC. Celtic swords and three-ribbed arrows of Scythian type were among the finds of weapons.

An extremely valuable find at Buneşti was the hoard of silver objects unearthed in 1979. This consisted of fourteen Thracian-type fibulae, two silver octagonal-band bracelets with free ends, two silver and bronze spiral wire bracelets with snakes at the end, a representative ornament of Geto-Dacian art, and fifteen conic-ending rings and a silver drachma minted in the city of Histria at the turn of the fourth century BC. The coin was deposited with the rest of the hoard probably for the quality of the silver in which it had been struck. The presence of the coin underlines the important role which Histria played in that region, as shown by the other discoveries of Histrian coins made at Obirşeni, Bîrlad, Găbeşti, Vaslui and Poiana, all situated in the same area. The Thracian-type fibulae found at Buneşti feature a faceted pin identical in form with the ones discovered in 1922 at Epureni-Huşi.

During the archaeological excavations of 1981 four pieces of silver put together were retrieved from a dwelling ; two were silver bracelets ending with sake heads, and two were Thracian-type fibulae with hammered pins of the same shape as those in the first hoard. Bronze ornaments identical with the silver ones were obtained from other dwellings. Alongside Thracian-type fibulae,

Celtic-type bronze and iron fibulae were also found at Buneşti.

The finds included glass paste beads on a blue background with white spots and a blue point in the middle, beads decorated with undulating yellow lines on a blue background, and four anthropomorphic masks painted in blue and black, these being similar to Celtic discoveries made in Transylvania, at Aţel-Bratei (Sibiu county), Fîntînele (Bistriţa-Năsăud county), Pişcolt (Satu Mare county) and Mangalia, in Dobrudja, dating back to the fourth to second centuries BC. There was a large circulation of these masks at the time. They had been known since the Hallstatt age in the Carpathian-Danubian-Pontic area, as was proved by discoveries at Ferigele (Vîlcea county). They had been brought to Romania in exchange dealings, first of all with Greek merchants.

Further research in Buneşti in 1982 led to the discovery of a second big hoard consisting of ornaments which had been stored in a Dacian cup with a slightly elevated handle and covered by an open-socket axle, a form known at this place from previous discoveries. In the hoard were a seventy-five-beaded amber necklace, a necklace with seventy pieces of coral, two silver-wire bracelets ending in animal heads, a bronze circular piece and two Cowrie shells, one of them in pieces. At that time amber beads had featured in only a few discoveries (Orlea, Piscolt), and up to the present no other ornaments containing coral pieces have been found on Romanian territory. The importance of this hoard is in its connection with the two tool storehouses nearby, their disposition (axes with the blades oriented in two precise directions) leading to the conclusion that their burial could very well have been of a votive character.

Half a metre below the surface a pot containing cult objects was unearthed. They were six idols of the Poiana type made of clay, a miniature clay vessel and two conic pieces also made of clay. The vessel that contained them was a medium-sized, bell-shaped pot, hand-turned in brown-reddish paste. Its decoration was made up of four prominences with a groove in the middle, between which a very carefully achieved notched band was displayed. A similar vessel, dating back to the first century BC, has been discovered so far only in the big archaeological site of Poiana (Galaţi county). Possibly it had been buried, just as the one at Buneşti had, in the course of religious practices in the Dacian world.

In analogy with other older discoveries at Buneşti, and in other settlements on Romanian territory, the deposits described here can be dated back to the late fourth century and early second century BC.

In the north of Moldavia, at Miculinţi, on the site where the Stînca-Costeşti hydroelectric power station was built (on the River Prut, Botoşani county), archaeologists led by Dr Mihai Brudiu, from the Galaţi County History Museum, have uncovered a settlement dating back nineteen thousand years to the height of the glaciary period. Excavations have proved that the inhabitants of the settlement, which contained many huts, were hunters of reindeer and wild horses and also fished with harpoons in the Prut. They used to make ingenious flint, bone and wooden tools and hunting weapons.

Numerous pieces have been discovered at Miculinţi which, according to their finders, are unique, on both a national and a world plane. The spears, for instance, had two grooves on their points, and this type, invented here, was widely copied elsewhere and is perpetuated to this day. Out of split reindeer antlers the hunters made harpoons of a special shape which chronologically, are the oldest in Europe and possibly in the world. Various tools and artefacts made of wood, which has become petrified, have been found in the settlement, and their preservation in this form has enabled researchers to study the uses to which they were put.

Another occupation of the inhabitants of the Miculinţi settlement was quarrying and working flint with reindeer-horn tools, reinforced with rock. These formed the first pickaxes in the world, used for excavating flint from a nearby quarry. The flint was shaped into various tools, such as chisels and scrapers, with which the local people worked antler, bone and wood to obtain other tools for hunting and fishing and making clothes from animal skins.

6. The Hinova Treasure

The vast works of reconstruction in modern Romania have resulted in archaeologists being sent to sites to see what can be discovered before the area is submerged under a sea of concrete or some similarly solid substance. On 20 July 1980 a team was working in a flat cremation cemetery in the area of the Iron Gates II hydroelectric power station on the Danube without any great hopes of a spectacular find because the cemetery was one in which the common people of a Thracian tribe, as opposed to the chieftain and other dignitaries, were buried. But when they opened an earthen vessel which could have been a funerary urn they found instead of human remains a fabulous golden treasure, hidden probably by a goldsmith more than three thousand years ago. It was a near miracle that the treasure came to light at such a late date because it was in an area where a Roman *castrum* was built in the third to fifth centuries AD : had the builders of this stronghold laid out the walls of the towers only thirty centimetres further south, the vessel and its rich contents would never have reached us.

The treasure may have been hidden during the great migrations of the Dorians and the Phrygian Thracians who, from the thirteenth century BC, infiltrated this territory, coming from the northern regions down to continental Greece and its islands, as well as to Asia Minor. During these migrations the inhabitants of the respective areas had no choice but to take shelter until the danger was over.

It was probably under these circumstances that the Hinova goldsmith buried the treasure, which included unfinished pieces, in order to find it upon his return. Had he decided to abandon it, he would hardly have chosen such a secure place. He would have known that, had he hidden it in the grave of a prince, it could have attracted the attention of the grave-looters who frequently accompanied every migration. The place chosen for shelter was the flat cremation cemetery usually reserved for ordinary people, because who would seek for a treasure there? Furthermore, the earthen vessel which sheltered the treasure looked no different from the funerary urns used by the population of those times during their burial rituals. But, for reasons which we can never know, the goldsmith never returned and the products of his workshop remained undisturbed in the earth.

The indications are that at Hinova, which is near the old Roman centre of Drobeta Turnu-Severin, there was a local workshop which specialized in the production of gold and bronze ornaments. Its emergence reflects the existence of a traditional skill in the processing of precious metals when it is remembered that excavations conducted in the same area exposed yet another treasure, the one at Ostrovul Mare, dated to a previous period, that of maximum development of the Bronze Age.

The weight of the pieces, nearly five thousand grams, proves that the Hinova workshop did not produce for one person alone but for a whole social category which had started differentiating itself within the Thraco-Getic society, namely the military and religious aristocracy. That aristocracy enjoyed exceptional economic and other privileges during this period. Judging by the splendour and richness revealed by the finds, their status was not different from that of the Mycenaean chieftains. Taking into account the fact that the Hinova finds date from a period of time close to the Trojan War, we can better understand what Homer meant when he so frequently mentions the exceptional wealth of Thracian chieftains. This must have been the light in which the contemporaries of the Thracian chieftain of Hinova looked upon him when he stood before them adorned with necklaces, bracelets and the other jewels of the treasure. It must have been so, because the Hinova treasure, which is now in the Museum of National History, Bucharest, does not represent an isolated find. Similar pieces, showing equally high skills, have been discovered all over the Carpatho-Danubian-Pontic area. The similarities between the finds at Hinova and those uncovered in many other parts throughout Romanian territory bear witness to the unity of the material and artistic culture which characterized the Thraco-Dacian society. This artistic tradition still continues, as is shown by the fact that the rhomboidal shapes in one the necklaces, to be described later, can be found in Romanian wooden architecture even today.

The gold of the Hinova treasure, which is believed to have come from the rich deposits of Dacia, probably Transylvania, was of exceptional quality. Analyses carried out by specialists of the National Bank have indicated that all the pieces contained in the treasure are of exceptional purity. The maker of these pieces must have possessed highly specialized skills. A sizeable part of the treasure consists of wires, remains of gold and fragments of ornaments that were intended for further reprocessing, assembled in balls of gold wire. Modern specialists examining the find found themselves confronted with an unusual situation. One of these balls of gold wire was made up of three different pieces, yet in all the three fragment-analyses conducted by experts of the National Bank with the most sophisticated instruments showed an identical content of gold. How this was achieved by a goldsmith working more that three thousand years ago without elaborate instruments at his disposal remains a mystery.

The treasure included a diadem made of a thin gold leaf, one millimetre thick, 59 centimetres long, 2.5 centimetres wide (in the middle) and 1.5 centimetres at the ends, weighing 20.652 grams. The whole surface was divided into sections, with the same ornament, which consisted of dotted circles surrounded by a continuous garland featuring various solar symbols. This decoration was widespread towards the end of the Bronze Age on metal objects but most particularly on the pottery discovered throughout the Geto-Dacian area. The same ornamental motif can be found on the disc-shaped *phalerae* (a smooth, shining ornament for the breast, a metal disc or boss) found in the fabulous hoard containing gold ornaments discovered in 1974 at Ţigănaşi (Mehedinţi), known as the treasure of Ostrovul Mare. Analogies to the decoration on the Hinova diadem can also be found in the *phalerae* of the treasures discovered at Tufalău (Covasna), which is dated to the end of the Bronze Age, at Săculeni (Bihor) and at Vărşand (Arad).

The treasure also included a muff-shaped bracelet made of gold leaf 5.2 centimetres wide. It has a round, slightly flattened shape and is 8.4 centimetres in diameter. The muff, which weighs 580.3 grams, was produced by hammering. It is similar, in some respects, to two gold cylindrical muffs, kept in the National Bank of Romania, whose place of origin is unknown. This type of bracelet was characteristic of the middle and late Bronze Age, being widespread particularly in Central Europe. Two bronze specimens, both similar to the gold one, have been discovered at Cehălut (Satu Mare) in the Someş plain in Transylvania.

Two spiral bracelets were also discovered in the Hinova treasure. One weighed 261.55 grams and the other 497.13 grams. The first, made of a thinner and narrower gold leaf, had a decoration consisting of two furrows cut along the edges, which were separated by a median crest. This type of bracelet also had its origins in the Bronze Age. The deposit of bronze objects found at Sînnicolau (Bihor) contains a metal bracelet with a similar furrow along the median line, dating from the second period of the Bronze Age (the Otomani culture, characteristic of the Banat and Crişana) which shows some similarities to the gold spiral bracelet discovered at Hinova. Among the variants of this type of bracelet are the spiral bracelet of bronze sheet found in the deposit of Săpînţa (Maramureş), which is dated to the middle Bronze Age, as well as the one at Maglavit (Olt), which dates from the fifteenth and fourteenth centuries BC. Two similar pieces made of spirally twisted gold are kept in the collections of the National Museum, but their place of origin is not known. The second spiral bracelet was made from a massive gold bar, showing, after hammering, six crests. After being beaten, the bar was twisted six times in order to take the required shape. It weighs 497.13 grams and presents analogies to a spiral bracelet that has been found in a deposit of bronze objects at Oradea which is dated to the end of the second period of the Bronze Age. The tradition of such ornaments was continued later on, as is indicated by the discovery of similar pieces at Balta Verde (Mehedinţi) which date from the Iron Age (eighth to sixth centuries BC).

Three open bracelets were found, weighing 202.7 grams, 92.1 grams and 39.47 grams respectively. The first type of bracelet was in a round, slightly ellipsoidal shape, showing, after hammering, eight crests, and the second type, made in the shape of a deformed circle, although belonging to the open bracelet category, had two ends which almost touched each other. Researchers point out that pieces similar to these two types are quite frequently contained in precious-metal treasure-troves, as well as in those containing bronze objects. Their presence in the treasures discovered in Transylvania at Birchiş, Sacoşul Mare, Meseşeni and Căuas IV (Satu Mare) points to the fact that craftsmen of the late Bronze and the early Hallstatt Ages had a marked preference for this type of bracelet. The third piece, made of a gold wire five millimetres thick, shows analogies to the objects found in the north-eastern part of Transylvania, such as the bronze deposits discovered at Domneşti, Cehălut and Valea lui Mihai (Bihor).

Among the bracelets were an ellipsoidal one and a closed one, both made by the hammering of a gold leaf. The closed bracelet, which weighed fifty-two grams, was decorated with four incised lines disposed lengthwise. On either side of these four lines the decoration is completed with obliquely disposed incisions. Two specimens similar to the ellipsoidal bracelet but made of bronze were discovered at Ghilod (Timiş).

Six spiral bracelets of double gold wire were discovered, two larger and four smaller. The largest of them weighed nearly a hundred grams and the second largest 87.90 grams. Gold spiral bracelets of this type have been discovered in Transylvania and the Banat, spanning a long period of time, which begins with the very late phase of the Bronze Age and ends with the middle Hallstatt. Similar pieces, but made of bronze, were discovered in the deposit of bronze objects at Sacoţ-Slătioara (Vîlcea).

One category of pieces of great artistic value is represented by the component elements of what are described as "earrings necklaces", presumably pieces which could be worn as earrings but which, when threaded together, formed a necklace on a gold string. One necklace of this type contained forty-five pieces. Most of these "earrings" were made from a piece of gold wire six millimetres thick and one centimetre long. No other pieces similar to this type of necklace have so far been discovered.

Another necklace consists of forty-seven bells of similar shape but of different sizes, weighing 223.05 grams. The decoration of the bells, or *tutuli*, is a simple one, consisting of two incised circles at the base of the funnel. The same motif is repeated around the wide cone-shaped mouth of the funnel. Judging by their size, these bells are believed to have made up a necklace, with the larger specimens in the middle and the smaller ones towards the ends, threaded on a thin gold string in such a way as to fit into others like funnels. The bells were produced by hammering, and upon a close inspection each funnel shows traces of an incomplete welding. Gold pieces of this type are rather rare. The closest analogy to the *tutuli* discovered at Hinova may be found in the bells that were found in the Cioclovina cave (Hunedoara). There are, however, some differences between them in the sense that the ones discovered at Cioclovina have, each of them, four triangular openings. Unlike those of Hinova, which served as adornments to a great chief of the time, the *tutuli* of Cioclovina are believed to have been mere pieces of trappings.

A most important item in the treasure consisted of a necklace made of 255 rhomboidal longitudinally perforated beads of different sizes and weights, a model passed on from one generation to another, which inspired Brâncuși when he produced his Infinite Column. The large number of pieces and their total weight (1108.65 grams) leads to speculation that the beads were produced for several necklaces. The beads are without decoration, their rhomboidal shape less often found in necklaces made of metal (bronze or gold) beads than in those with beads made of other substances. Nevertheless, the large deposit of bronze objects discovered in the Cioclovina cave contained, among other things, 3,043 "pearls" (beads), of which a thousand were of amber and came in various sizes, quite similar to those found at Hinova. These pieces can be dated to the first period of the Hallstatt — this lasted up to the eighth century BC.

A hoard of gold "pearls" of the spindle type was in the Hinova treasure in two categories. The first included some twenty specimens, with a height ranging from five millimetres to 2.4 centimetres. The highest piece was massive, with a diameter (2.5 centimetres) exceeding its height and was in the shape of two truncated cones. The twenty specimens made up a necklace with a total weight of 101.25 grams. The second category of "pearls", also in the shape of two truncated cones, included 486 pieces and had a total weight of 146.06 grams. The "pearls", 3.5 millimetres high, were hollow and could be threaded on a string or thin gold wire. They are thought to have been produced by hammering. A comparison may be made with the specimens discovered in the deposit of bronze objects at Cioclovina. The deposit uncovered at Ulmi-Liteni (Jassy in Moldavia) contained nineteen beads made of glassy paste ; these were very similar to the

gold ones found at Hinova. Seven massive and beautifully
polished gold "pearls" of the spindle type were found in
the treasure discovered in Argeş county. Believed to be
contemporaneous with the *phalerae* of Ostrovul Mare, the
Argeş "pearls" may have been the component elements
of another necklace.

Among the less important discoveries at Hinova were
many very small beads in the shape of a conehead, four
cylindrical muffs similar to those found in the Turnu
Măgurele treasure, and four rings of double gold wire
spirals. The solitary bronze object was a bracelet for
whose casting a bivalved mould was used. This type of
bracelet was widespread during the late Bronze Age and
the early Hallstatt. Similar bronze bracelets of the same
period have been unearthed at Domăneşti, Moftinul Mic
and Satu Mare (all in Satu Mare county).

The jeweller's workshop at Hinova has not so far been
discovered but we have some idea of the contents of a
Dacian workshop of a later date from excavations at
Pecica in Transylvania. These included three bar-casting
moulds, two valves for the casting of rings, two large iron
anvils, eight small bronze chisels and five crucibles.

7. The Princely Tomb at Cugir

One of the most dramatic finds relating to the last years of Dacian independence is that of the grave of a high military chief in the fortress hill at Cugir (Alba county in Transylvania). The geographer Ptolemy (second century BC), when listing the most important cities in Dacia, placed one of them, Singidava, on the Mureş, near Apulum (Alba Iulia today). This might be the great Dacian settlement discovered at Cugir. Specialists know, from excavations, that the hill was already inhabited in the Bronze Age and that a second settlement on the site followed in the early Iron Age.

In Dacian times extensive works were carried through for building the terraces which surround the higher plateau and especially for consolidating the plateau. At that time big defence ramparts were erected with earth and stone as well as high walls of local stone and river boulders. Clay was used as binding material. In certain parts holes were carved in the rock for the walls, while other portions of the rock were preserved as buttresses.

During the excavations specialists were able to establish the times of the last two phases of habitation : one started in the third century BC and the second, dating from the first century BC, lasted until AD 106, the year of the defeat of King Decebalus by the Emperor Trajan. It was then destroyed by a strong fire, probably lit by the victorious Romans. The epoch of the great Dacian King Burebista, represented by the Cugir fortress, shows that it was a time of a flourishing economy, as reflected by finds of imported products from the Greek and Roman worlds. The importance of the settlement is also proved by two large silver hoards discovered in its perimeter. Each consists of over two thousand silver coins, minted locally and imitating those of Macedonia and Greece.

The cemetery of the settlement was on the south-west side of the hill on a slope so steep that one can hardly believe that tumuli could be built there in ancient times. Rainwater washed the tumuli away in the course of two thousand years but the graves remained. Among them was a remarkable one dated to the first century BC, therefore of the time of Burebista, and containing the remains of a great warrior, or chieftain, whose name has not been recorded. Specialists have established that a terrace over eight metres wide was dug in the hill where the burial took place in a ceremony described by none of the ancient authors and which is difficult for us to visualize today. In the centre of the terrace there is a small oval hollow more than one metre in diameter over which was erected the funeral pyre, made of big beams of fir wood and other woods yet to be established.

On the pyre the mourners placed a wonderful triumphal car on which lay the dead warrior dressed in combat armour. Horses, slaughtered for the ceremony, were harnessed to the car. The number is uncertain but over a hundred kilograms of calcinated bones were collected. The custom of slaughtering horses for the burial of a great personage was widespread in the Thracian world.

The fire must have been very strong since it burned the whole surface of the terrace to brick colour. When it died away and the ashes were still hot, everything that was left was piled in the central hollow over which the pyre had been erected and covered with a clay layer. When the clay came into contact with the hot metal or the hot ashes, it was burnt and became hardened. Then a beautiful bronze vessel (*situla*) made in Italy (in the Campagnia), was placed in the centre with over it a wonderful Dacian fruit bowl, 0.70 metres in diameter, and above all this a huge boulder. Finally, a tumulus was erected with earth and boulders.

In the pile of ashes on the funeral pyre archaeologists have discovered the metal remains of the car and of the wheels, numerous bronze and iron ornaments from the car and harness as well as the arms and dress of the dead man. He wore a wonderful, richly ornamented Hellenic iron helmet and iron armour adorned with rosettes. For weapons, he had a long sword, an iron-headed spear, a shield with an iron edge and handle (*umbo*) and the specifically Dacian dagger with a curved blade. The gold-plated harness was adorned with animal motifs, of which only a few were preserved.

The Dacian princely grave at Cugir has helped to answer many of the problems posed by the Dacian civilization. It has added to the other princely graves discovered in the vicinity of other settlements outside the Carpathian arch such as Popeşti, Brad, Răcătău, Radovanu, Piscu Crăsani and Cetăţeni, but nowhere else have such a well-preserved tomb and such a rich inventory been unearthed.

This short chapter has been compiled from an article by Dr I. H. Crişan in *Pages of History* and from a paper on the princely tomb he gave to the third international symposium on the Thracians at Palma in Majorca in 1981. In this paper he pointed out that chance can be an important factor in archaeology. This tomb was discovered when an emplacement for an anti-aircraft gun was being prepared. Dr Crişan is critical of the way in which the conquered Dacians are portrayed in Trajan's Column in Rome : in scanty clothing without armour and metal helmets. I myself have noticed the scanty clothing of the local population as shown on the monument at Adamclisi. Dr Crişan considers that the theme of the sculptures on Trajan's Column "constitutes an act of propaganda for the emperor and the empire", without value as a true historical document. The Dacian society, he said, was profoundly stratified and had attained a high level of development. When the Roman armies under Trajan conquered Dacia, they did not find before them a barbarous people but one with a high degree of civilization, of which the princely tomb of Cugir was evidence.

8. Excavations near Brașov and the First Romanian School

A map in the Museum of History and Archaeology in Brașov shows the sites of the hundreds of excavations carried out in the town and county, particularly the latter, in the past fifteen years. Although Brașov, which was already occupied in the neolithic era, is set in a mountainous area, most of the settlements are in the basin of the Olt river which flows through Brașov county but not through the town. In an area eighty kilometres square there are eight hundred archaeological sites (most of them closed) ; the great bulk are north-west of the town but there are twenty sites south and south-west. In Brașov itself there were six Dacian settlements and four occupied by Daco-Romans.

I examined the map with Dr Florea Costea, Deputy Director of the Museum and chief archaeologist there. He explained that in the course of excavations he did not find any period following Trajan's victory in which there was not evidence of Dacian or Daco-Roman life. Discoveries dated from paleolithic and neolithic times. Three archaeologists worked from Brașov, and during the season they were joined by others from Bucharest and Cluj-Napoca, so that at any one time ten archaeologists might be in the field. A single site might have forty workers supervised by an archaeologist. Most sites were discovered during the course of ploughing but others resulted from aerial photography.

One of the most important sites was at Felmer, eighty-four kilometres from Brașov, where excavations started in 1981. Settlements there dated from neolithic times through to the arrival of Saxon settlers in the twelfth century. Two Dacian settlements were found, two other villages where Roman colonists had settled, and a fifth where Romans and Dacians had lived together. The discoveries included stone monuments, kilns where ceramics were made, others where Romans separated iron ore, and coins with inscriptions.

In Şercaia, fifty-one kilometres from Braşov and fifteen from Făgăraş, the first big commune of Făgăraş land met on the Braşov-Sibiu highway, researchers found that in one square kilometre fifty-eight Daco-Roman families once lived in one settlement and this was one of thirty-three such villages in the area.

Excavations showed that at Dumbraviţa there was a Dacian settlement before the first century, a Daco-Roman one in the third and fourth centuries, and, with the mixing of the two races, a Romanian village in the ninth and tenth centuries.

There are two Daco-Roman settlements at Hărman, a commune eleven kilometres north of Braşov, twenty-five settlements in Rotbav, a commune standing on the banks of the Olt in the Racoş defile twenty-three kilometres from Braşov, three at Jibert, and three at Rupea, sixty-five kilometres from Braşov, of which one was Roman. Nearer Braşov, ceramics of the third and fourth centuries were unearthed at Feldiora, a locality situated on a hillock on which there was a Roman *castrum*.

One of Dr Costea's maps showed a sector in Braşov county where excavations revealed eleven Roman settlements, fourteen occupied jointly by Daco-Romans and twenty-five that dated from between the fourth and twelfth centuries. He told me that two sites had been left unexcavated so that anyone who doubted his findings could excavate them for himself and thereby confirm his conclusions about dating and other matters.

An in-depth study of one particular village, Comana de Jos, has been carried out by Dr Costea and two colleagues, I. Glodariu and I. Ciupea. They point out that the archaeological research enterprises at Comana de Jos resulted from the need to investigate archaeologically the area limited by the mountains of Perşani and Făgăraş and by the course of the River Olt, a historic zone known under the name of "Făgăraş country". Also, the big hydroelectric works which were planned and involved the course of the Olt, affecting certain places of archaeological interest, made research a matter of urgency.

The researchers point out that excavations in the perimeter of the commune of Comana de Jos resulted in the identification of many homes of different epochs. Houses of the Iron Age were found on Dealul Slătinii and on Dealul Heleşteului, both north-east of the village, on the left of the road which goes to Rupea ; the two hills formed high terraces on the left bank of the Olt. Four kilns on Dealul Heleșteului were discovered with ceramics which dated to the eighth and ninth centuries (AD). Other ceramics, in fragments, dating from the fourth century, were found in a field south-west of the village. Archaeological material from the time of the Dacians had been found at Pleșița Pietroasă, a hill sixteen hundred metres from Comana de Jos. Other discoveries related to the period of Roman occupation. Even at the time of the Emperor Aurelian, the population was already Daco-Roman. Most of the material discovered during excavations on the hill of Comana de Jos consisted of ceramics which came under three categories : those made by hand, by the wheel and by the fast wheel. In the opinion of the researchers, based on the shape and decoration of the vessels, they came from homes in Comana de Jos which existed there in the eighth century, possibly at the end of the previous century and probably continued into the ninth century. Dr Costea told me that excavations would continue in Comana de Jos so that the contents of cemeteries could be examined. This district had a large population in Dacian times and was heavily fortified. In 1984 researchers had discovered two Dacian fortresses, one in Racos twenty-one metres long and another in Bogata, but the latter had not yet been excavated.

A characteristic of the Dacian settlements in the south-east of Transylvania is the fact that most of them are situated in open fields — an obvious pointer to agriculture and cattle-raising having been the main pursuits of the inhabitants. Most settlements had no defence walls or ditches. This was because the Carpathian arc provided one of the most efficient natural defences. There were, however, some fortresses surrounded by walls which were intended to be used as places of refuge by the population in the case of possible penetration by the enemy into the narrow valleys of the mountains. These fortresses did not make up a defence system such as the one set up by the Romans on the boundaries of the Empire. This can be explained by the fact that the region lying on the other side of the Carpathians was inhabited by a Geto-Dacian population. These fortresses convey the impression of a system characteristic of a state made up of several tribes, each enjoying a certain measure of independence.

One of the principal fortresses is at Covasna, north-east of Braşov. It stands on a mountain peak with three terraces and is surrounded by a wall made of stone slabs set with mud. The walls are very thick, their width ranging between 3.5 and nine metres. Finds here include pottery (hand-made and wheel-worked) consisting of vessels, jars, goblets, cups and fruit dishes decorated with alveolate or incised bands. There were also household utensils and weapons specific to the Geto-Dacians. Particular interest has been aroused by the coins discovered on one of the terraces. The Roman republican denarii found here indicate that the fortress was already in existence in the first century BC, a time of maximum development of the Geto-Dacian state. Another coin was issued in AD 72, at the time of the Emperor Vespasian. The end of the fortress was brought about by a huge fire which charred the earth near the walls as well as some of its stones. Possibly the victorious Romans were responsible for the destruction of the fortress.

Another fortress in the Covasna district was at the village of Valea Seacă, situated on a stone promontory standing in a lateral valley of the Casin rivulet. The fortress can be approached only from the north. The plateau of the promontory was dug into two terraces which are surrounded by a stone wall bound with unburnt clay. The wall is 1.8 metres thick, and the dimensions of the oval-shaped fortress are forty-five by twenty-five metres. It was built on the foundations of a former Thracian fortress dated to the Bronze Age. The large number of pottery fragments, characteristic of the second Iron Age, prove that the period of maximum development of the fortress spanned the first century BC and the first century AD. A complex of dwellings was discovered in the vicinity. In times of danger the people from this settlement could seek refuge in the fortress up on the cliff.

At Angheluş, a settlement in the Covasna district, discoveries include a mould in which jewels, particularly amphora-shaped pendants, were cast. This indicates that a handicraft centre, where ornaments for a wider area were made, was in operation there.

Another settlement in the Covasna district was Cernat, the site of an important trading centre where imported goods, especially Greek pottery, were traded. Among the more important objects discovered was a bowl to which a stamp with Greek letters had been applied. A fragment of a decorated vessel featuring a procession of girls

carrying offerings was also found. This vessel belonged
to the so-called Pergamon pottery and originated in the
city of Mismekion in the Crimean Peninsula. The settlement at Cernat came into existence before the second century BC and continued to prosper until the first century
AD, as is indicated by the local imitations of the drachmas issued under Alexander of Macedonia which were
discovered in one of the dwellings.

A settlement discovered at Poiana (Covasna district)
spanned the same period of time as the one at Cernat.
Among the objects found there were the bronze fibulae
with a spiral-shaped spring, a type characteristic of the
Geto-Dacian civilization.

Braşov has the distinction of having the first Romanian
school in the country, built in the grounds of the church
of St Nicolae (Nicholas) and opened in 1399. As it was
outside the fortress of Braşov, the church and school
authorities feared that it would be destroyed and during
the Middle Ages buried it under earth. The work of
excavation started in 1912 and finished in 1950, through
the interruption of the two world wars. The original
wooden building had been rebuilt in stone in 1495.
Professor Faust Remus, director of the museum which
incorporates the old school and its belongings, explained
that the school opened with one room and thirty pupils,
mostly belonging to the families of rulers, and was
extended until there were six rooms and 180 pupils,
including some from Wallachia and Moldavia. The
teachers were priests, and the school included a chapel.

The school helped to fulfil national aspirations by
incorporating a printing press in the building : it was
here that the oldest printing machine in Romania was
installed in 1557, the printer being Diaconul (Deacon)
Coresi and the first book printed being one on anatomy.
Other books in Romanian followed, but the object of
having a printing press in the school was primarily for
the production of schoolbooks.

What is so unusual about this school is that it has
been restored to show what it was like when it was first
opened, giving an impression of austerity with its plain
wooden seats, but this is offset by the display of gifts
from rulers, including a cross with diamonds given by
Michael the Brave when he visited the school in 1600,
found on the site during the excavations. Other exhibits
include icons painted on metal. Among the valuable
books and documents is a copy of the score of the first

Romanian operetta *Crai Nou (New Saint)*, composed by Ciprian Porumbescu in 1882.

Braşov is well worth a visit. Apart from the chance to see sites being worked during the season, there is the permanent display of more than eight thousand items, most of them of archaeological interest, in the town's museum in the main square a building which, because of its tower, gives the impression of being a church. However, the tower, fifty-eight metres high, was erected between 1525 and 1528 to serve as a watchtower, and what is now the museum was once the council hall where, centuries ago, the hundred leaders of the town gathered. Another museum is that of the Braşov Citadel in the Weavers' Bastion, the best preserved of the seven bastions of the town's fortifications. The citadel museum displays examples of the work of the guilds, tools, arms and armour, documents and coins.

9. The Ceramics Factory beneath the Potato Patch

One of the most touching exhibits in the Brukenthal Museum in Sibiu is the tombstone of a family of the second or third centuries from Apoldul de Sus, Sibiu county, with carvings of a Roman husband and Dacian wife, the difference being made clear by their dress and features. The Dacian woman's dress has a well-sculpted fibula on it, with a fibula of the same type on display in another room. The small heads of their four children are also sculpted on the tombstone. Possibly they pre-deceased their parents. More than anything else, such a tombstone provides proof of the mingling of the two races from the time of the Roman conquest.

In the same room as the tombstone there are small oil lamps with the sign of the cross and the name of the maker in Latin, of a type found in different sites in the Sibiu area, dating from the end of the fourth century, and ceramics for the production of greetings cards in the same era. It is possible to follow the development of ceramics from the fourth to the eleventh century in this museum. Most of the exhibits were found in Bratei, Gusterita, Seica Mica, Sura Mica and Ocna Sibiului. Some came from Boita, south of Sibiu.

Sibiu, like Brașov, is a fortified town with links going back to neolithic times and, in a later period of history, had a strong Saxon population. Even today a question in the street in German is more likely to be answered than one in English. A map in the archaeological section of the museum shows nearly fifty archaeological sites west of Șercaia, most of them south and east of Sibiu and relating to the neolithic period, and a significant number have yielded items that throw light on the people who lived in this part of Transylvania after Aurelian withdrew his legions. For instance, in Biertan, eighty kilometres north of Sibiu, researchers have found evidence of occupation from before Roman times up to the tenth century AD. These consist mainly of ceramics and coins but they include the celebrated bronze *donarium*, a Christian votive item, a photograph of which is in the museum (the original is on display in Bucharest).

The exhibits in this museum were shown to me by Professor Claudia Cerchez, and her remarks were expanded by Dr Iuliu Paul, Professor of Archaeology at the University of Sibiu who is a specialist at the museum. Proof of settlement in this area between the second and tenth centuries is contained in twenty-five settlements discovered in the county of Sibiu alone. Excavations at Bratei near Mediaş since 1955 have uncovered four settlements dating from the third to the tenth century, including three cemeteries, one of the fourth century, another from the eighth and a third which belonged to the Gepidae. Dr Paul told me that in order to foil grave-robbers the Gepidae were in the habit of collecting treasures and other belongings of the deceased in a bag which was placed between the feet, the thinking behind this being that the robber, not finding precious objects on the body, would assume that there was nothing to steal. At Sura Mica, close to Ocna Sibiului, sixteen kilometres north-west of Sibiu, two settlements excavated covered an area of about ten hectares, the first being from the late Roman period and the second from the fourth to the seventh century.

Professor Paul took me to Slimnic, north of Sibiu, where six sites have been excavated, revealing that people lived there in the Roman period. Although inter-marriage had already started between Dacians and Romans after the Roman victory in AD 106, there was evidence of both cultures. Researchers also found objects such as vases, ceramics, farming implements, brooches and rings which dated from the fourth to the seventh century. Although the two cultures were distinctive, it was clear that assimilation took place. Migrations had passed through this area but the culture of the Daco-Romans had remained unchanged. It was difficult to realize, as we stood in gentle countryside, that the fields had been disturbed by excavations, but this was evidence of the care taken to restore sites to their former condition so that agriculture would not be adversely affected. The harvest had been gathered in and during July the sites would be reopened, with between forty and sixty workers, mostly students, engaged in excavations under the supervision of two archaeologists.

We continued north, passing Rusi, where two settlements dating from the fourth century had been discovered, to Seica Mica, where settlements on both sides of the road showed that people had lived there between the fourth and ninth centuries, the evidence for this being ceramics and agricultural tools. These sites are still being developed and more finds are expected.

Our journey, which took us well on the way to Medias, ended at Micasasa, a village of three thousand people, where we were escorted to a potato patch in the church garden. There was nothing of an archaeological nature to be seen here but I was assured that beneath our feet there had been a Daco-Roman settlement, discovered in 1975, when excavations had started. Not only had a great many ceramics of the third and fourth centuries been discovered but photographs were produced to show that the site contained a ceramics factory at a depth of ten metres. Over a hundred houses had once stood here. Many coins discovered on the site helped to establish the period. The Tîrnava Mare river flowed nearby, and Professor Paul pointed out that the serious floods of 1977 had revealed a tomb which indicated the site of a cemetery which still had to be excavated.

The former Roman road from Sibiu had run through Micasasa to Alba Iulia, where in 1980 an important archaeological discovery brought to light new evidence of the continuation of the life of the inhabitants of this area after the withdrawal of the Roman legions and administration. When a burial ground was excavated, 450 cremation and inhumation graves were found — 75 belonged to the second and third centuries, 195 to the seventh to tenth centuries and 180 to the eleventh and twelfth centuries. The inventory of the graves as well as the complete absence of weapons, proved that the graves belonged to a peaceful, sedentary population of land-tillers and animal-breeders, as the seventh to twelfth century Romanian population was. Dr Ştefan Pascu described the discovery of the graves as "one of the most valuable archaeological finds made in Romania during the last few years. This is the first time that such a large number of graves have been discovered in a limited area. Likewise, we have noted that the graves belong to various periods, lying over Roman graves. The finds at Alba Iulia elucidate numerous questions and bring new data regarding the history and continuity of the Romanian people. It is known that very few data about the seventh and eighth centuries were available. This was the main reason that made several foreign historians question the continuity of the Romanians in the Alba zone. This necropolis belies once and for all such erroneous theories."

When Dr Pascu wrote this excavations at Alba Iulia were still continuing. Eventually more than one thousand graves were found. Excavations have now finished.

The cemetery at Alba Iulia was discovered in the vicinity of the Roman *castrum*. Among the objects of archaeological interest brought to light were red and grey ceramics (similar to those discovered all over the area where the Romanian population lived), earrings, bracelets and rings. Dr Pascu described the discovery as a clear sign of the existence in this area of one of the most important Romanian *voivode*-ships in the eighth to eleventh centuries, long before the feudal Hungarian state conquered Transylvania. The Alba Iulia *voivode*-ship, known in the epoch by the name of Balgrad, was located in the middle Mureş basin in the centre of Romania, a zone rich in historical remains. Near these graves were three huts and the stone foundations of thirteen Roman houses with wood frameworks covered with tiles and hollow tiles. Two wells were found.

On the road back to Sibiu I discussed with Dr Paul the fact that the sites we had inspected had been in river valleys, which hardly suggested fear of invaders, but he pointed out that there was evidence that in times of invasion settlements tended to be found nearer mountains. Excavations had yielded a rich harvest of 140,000 items from sites but there was room for only five per cent of them in the archaeological section of the Brukenthal Museum. More room would be available when the new room was opened in 1986.

One of the most important sites in Transylvania is the large cemetery at Soporul de Cîmpie, dating to the second and third centuries, thirty kilometres north-east of antique Potaissa, now known as Turda, discovered by the archaeologist Dumitru Protase in the autumn of 1955 and excavated between then and 1961. He found there 193 tombs of the Daco-Roman period of which 25 were by burial of the body and 168 of ashes after the body had been incinerated. Only four bodies were those of adults; the rest were those of children less than seven years old.

The bodies that had been incinerated were in graves of three different categories: 137 had ashes contained in urns; twenty-six were in simple graves without urns; three of the graves contained ashes in an urn which stood on a small pedestal. Two of the urns were covered. The cremation of the bodies had been carried out on a special platform outside the cemetery. Some graves contained ashes in vases, presumably because urns were not available. The design and quality of the urns were different from one grave to another, depending on the age, wealth or sex of the deceased and the time when the burial was carried out. In nearly a hundred tombs typical Dacian pottery (urns, covers or lids, potsherds, fragments) was found mixed up with Roman pottery.

The cemetery contained Roman urns of superior quality with or without handles; urns of the Roman type, of low quality and made with the wheel, brown in colour and without handles; and Dacian urns without handles, dark-coloured, with the specific decorations of Dacian ceramics. Fragments of Dacian and Roman ceramics were found inside some urns, but other objects, such as jewels, drinking-vessels, rings, earrings, pearls, fibulae, pendants and coins, buried with the body or ashes, were never found in urns, proving that this was a habit and tradition well established by the Dacian population. The bronze coins found in the cemetery were from the reigns of rulers from Trajan (98-117) to Marcus Aurelius (160-80).

Dumitru Protase considered that the cemetery of Soporul de Cîmpie provided the clearest archaeological evidence of the persistence of the vanquished Dacians under Roman domination. The settlement which had used the cemetery had not been identified, he said.

A Dacian cup made during the Roman occupation of Dacia was found in 1959 in front of the Partizan Hotel in Horea Street, Cluj-Napoca, the capital city of Transylvania. Part of the cup which would have held the handle, had there been one, was missing, but researchers could not ascertain whether this cup was of the type with or without a handle. A similar cup, dated to the third century, was found in the cemetery at Soporul de Cîmpie, where it had been used to cover ashes in an urn. The Dacian cup at Cluj-Napoca was found with fragments of Roman vases. The oldest layer excavated here belonged to the Roman period; above it was a layer containing objects belonging to the feudal period. The material found in Horea Street, which is considered to be of great value, is in the archaeological museum in Cluj-Napoca.

Also in this museum are fragments of Roman and Dacian vases, hand-made, found at Ciunga in the commune of Ocna Mureş, in the Aiud region, in 1963 by the archaeologist Ion Mitrofan. They had some decorations in relief and a design round the brim. These fragments, found on the surface, proved that a settlement of the original population of Transylvania had existed at this spot at the time of the Roman occupation.

In a Roman camp at Gilău, near the town of Huedin, forty-eight kilometres from Cluj on the road to Oradea, a quantity of ceramics of Dacian origin was found with fragments of Roman provincial ceramics, proving that Dacians had almost certainly been inside the camp. Fragments of Dacian cups without handles found in the camp and in the surrounding countryside were similar to those found in the cemetery at Soporul de Cîmpie and other Dacian settlements of the second and third centuries in Transylvania. Fragments at Gilău came from about thirty-five different vases, the most common being the type in which grain was stored. The material used for Dacian vessels was different from that used by the Romans, the mixture not as pure and not as well finished. The Dacian ware was usually dark-coloured but some was red ; incomplete firing resulted in the colour being impure. They were mostly without decorations.

Important Roman provincial ceramics together with fragments of Dacian vases, among them a typical Dacian cup, were found at Noşlac, in the Aiud region, a local settlement, as was shown by animal bones and stones used for milling grain. Some of these finds, considered to be very valuable, are in the archaeological museum at Cluj-Napoca.

During excavation of a Roman *castrum* at Orheiul Bistriţei, in the Bistriţa region, by the Bistriţa museum staff in collaboration with the Institute of History at Cluj-Napoca, primitive hand-made Dacian ceramics were found together with rich and varied Roman archaeological material. The Dacian material consisted of fragments of seven or eight different types of ceramics, including three different cups, only one of which was whole, for holding candles. It was considered significant that Dacian ceramics were found with Roman objects *inside* the camp.

One of the most notable achievements of Dr Protase was to publish a survey of monetary finds and treasures relating to the period that followed the conquest of Dacia by the Romans up to AD 450. Writing in 1966, he said that we know today that nearly a hundred hoards of coins were buried on Dacian soil at the time of the Roman occupation, among which were thirty-four in which the most important pieces were from before the Roman conquest. Eleven piles of coins were collected by members of the same family, commencing with the period before the wars between Trajan and Decebalus and continuing during the occupation and organization of Dacia as a Roman province. Protase considers that the discovery of coins in post-Roman Dacia constitutes a valuable argument in favour of the existence of the original population when taken in conjunction with archaeological finds. If the coins were studied in isolation, they were not able to provide the necessary evidence for the degree of socio-economic development and commercial relations and exchanges between the population of different regions.

Dr Protase published a table showing finds of coins between the reigns of Aurelian and Theodosius II (408-50). Most of the discoveries were of coins issued between 306 and 392. This was determined principally by the political situation created by Constantine the Great, who reconquered for the Empire large territories north of the Danube from Wallachia to Banat, negotiated a durable peace with the Goths (332) and by his energetic measures revived the economy of the state. Among the finds of coins were ten discovered in Transylvania, nineteen in Banat and two in Oltenia.

Dr Protase points out that, when considering the problem of the continuity of the Roman element in the old province, it is necessary to give particular importance to the places where coins of the period from Aurelian to Theodosius II were found. They were discovered not only in certain zones but on the whole territory occupied by Daco-Romans. The great majority of the coins were made of bronze, very few of silver, and those of gold were extremely rare, proving that coins were not acquired for their intrinsic value but for use in exchanges. There was a difference between the customs of the local population, which used bronze coins that were of negligible value for their metal content, and those of the Goths, who valued coins for their content of precious metal. The proof of this was in treasures, such as those found at Șimleul Silvaniei, Crasna and Valea Strîmbă, which without doubt belonged to the Goths and which contained exclusively objects of gold, associated sometimes with gold and silver Roman coins.

Bronze and silver coins were often found in houses in Roman camps, rural settlements and the cemeteries of the original population established at the end of the third century and during the fourth century. An analysis of the circulation of coins between the years 271, when Aurelian withdrew his forces south of the Danube, and 450 led to the conclusion that (by their diffusion, the great frequency with which they were found and the collections of them in old rural settlements and urban and military centres in the province) coins constituted a valuable argument for the persistence of the Daco-Roman population in the regions of the left bank of the lower Danube and the interior of the Carpathian arc.

10. The Finds at Bratei

In 376 important contingents of Goths crossed the Danube and settled in the Empire. The imperial administration could not cope with the enormous problems raised by the newcomers, which led to the violent rebellion of the Visigoths who, in the Battle of Adrianopolis, decisively defeated the imperial armies (378). A few decades later, in 408, the Huns, led by Uldin, crossed the Danube, devastating the whole of Thracia. The population took refuge in Dalmatia. Immediately the Empire tried, by laws and edicts, to regulate the juridical situation of the newcomers.

In both cases the written sources of the epoch are rich in data and details referring to the migrants and especially to the major problems they raised. On the other hand, one century earlier (271-5), when an entire province was moved to the south of the Danube, as some historians assert, for this supposed event the information is so scanty as to be practically useless. A happening of exceptional importance was treated as news in brief. This represents the documentary basis of the theory of the abandonment and complete evacuation of Dacia's population, a theory born in the nineteenth century and continuously enriched with arguments lacking any direct or indirect documentary support. It may be asked where were the tens of thousands of Daco-Romans said to be south of the Danube at the end of the third and in the fourth century. The epigraphical and archaeological investigations undertaken south of the Danube do not identify the presence there of north Danubian Daco-Romans, but they were found north of the Danube on Oltenia's territory (the former Lower Dacia) and also in Transylvania (the former Dacia Superior).

The withdrawal of the administration and the army, accompanied to a certain extent by some rich strata of the population, was followed by the intensification of rural life and the diminution of the urban one, clearly shown by archaeological research. Thus it was found that, during the fourth century in Sarmizegetusa, capital of Dacia, the entrances of the amphitheatre were closed and the building was transformed into a place for refugees. The few graves found in Sarmizegetusa, together with numerous coins and bronze jewellery of the fourth century, offer valuable proof of the continuity of the population in this area of the Roman province. At Sarmizegetusa it has been proved that the medieval settlement, modest as to the number of inhabitants and as an area, maintained itself in the northwest corner of the fortified Roman town, the Roman streets serving, at the beginning of the Middle Ages and even until today, as lines for the streets of the village. This is the first example known on the territory of Romania of the conservation, in the structure of a medieval and contemporary settlement, of the plan of a part of a Roman settlement. There is little doubt that future researches will multiply such examples on the entire territory of Transylvania.

At Alba Iulia (ancient Apulum), the Daco-Roman population limited itself to certain zones of the former town. Bronze coins of the fourth century, jewellery, such as the well-known fibulae with buttons, and ceramics, provide evidence that in the fourth century this area was inhabited.

In Potaissa (Turda), one of the headquarters of the Roman army, the continuity of the population in the fourth century is eloquently illustrated by numerous bronze coins of this century. This was also the case in Cluj-Napoca and in the north of the province at Porolissum (Moigrad). Newer or older discoveries at Porolissum and surroundings attest the spread of Christianity in this corner of the former province. Among the finds are ceramics with a coral bottom specific to those of the Daco-Roman population of the fourth century.

The incomplete image we have of the life of the Daco-Roman population of urban areas of the fourth century is due to the early level of the investigations made in the former urban centres of Dacia. The results obtained so far indicate strong prospects for intensive future research on this cultural aspect of life in the fourth century.

Incomparably richer is the image of the rural scene.
The richness of the information relating to the countryside clearly reflects the intensification of the rural
life of the Daco-Roman population of the fourth century.
For instance, in Transylvania the number of settlements
discovered between 1966 and 1983 increased more than
four times. Researchers have identified in Transylvania
more than seventy settlements. Similar discoveries have
been made in Oltenia and in the fortresses along the
Danube. Of particular importance for the light they throw
on the life of the Daco-Roman population during the
fourth century are the rural settlements discovered at
Locusteni-Gropşani and Gropşani-Olt.

One of the most interesting populated areas of the
post-Roman period is the Tîrnava basin, which proved
to be intensively inhabited during the first millennium
AD. Isolated discoveries of the last century drew attention to this area. For instance, it is sufficient to mention the famous *donarium* of Biertan, in Sibiu county,
dating from the fourth century, together with bronze
vessels which belonged to a Christian dwelling. This *donarium* is a Christian votive item made of two bronze
plates: the upper one has an inscription reading *"I
Zenovius made this gift"* and the lower one Christ's
monogram in a circular medallion. The Biertan discovery
offers a valuable indication of the kind of Christianity
that existed without architectural monuments of stone
specific to the Roman groups.

But the most spectacular revelation is undoubtedly
represented by the discovery in 1956 of the Bratei
archaeological complex near Mediaş in Transylvania.
One cemetery at Bratei, datable to the fifth and sixth
centuries AD by its rite, ritual and inventory, is in
accordance with the best Roman provincial traditions.
The large number of graves investigated (367) dispels
any doubt about the general historical conclusions infer-
able from their analysis. A clear understanding of the
chronology and cultural position of this cemetery is
facilitated by the existence of one single culture layer,
that corresponding to its utilization, on the whole area
of the terrace. There is no element of material culture
datable before the year 275. Therefore the opportunity
to mix up elements of separate cultures, either because
of the complicated history of the place or because of the
researchers, inexpertise, is out of the question. The cemetery must have functioned in the fourth and very likely,

in the early fifth century. Three coins, one Constantius (337-40), one Valens (364-78), both burnt on the funeral pyre and one possibly Theodosius (379-95), have been found in the graves. Consideration of every detail compels the conclusion that the people who used to bury their dead in the cemetery at Bratei were a strong Daco-Illyro-Roman community which stubbornly preserved its pagan traditions until the beginning of the fifth century AD. In fact, the discontinuance of the cemetery was presumably due to the progress of evangelism in the fifth century. Strong indications of the persistence of spiritual and material traditions of the Daco-Romans until the first decades of the fifth century are found in this cemetery in such details as the laying of the cremation remains at the mouth of the hole, the fragmentary pottery, the large number of meat offerings, the presence of hearths explainable by the practice of burial feasts over the grave and the preference for certain categories of pottery.

Contents of the two cemeteries at Bratei include animal bones (ox, sheep, goats), stones, coals, jewellery (bronze and iron brooches, glass and amber necklaces), bone combs, glasses, grinding-mills of the Roman type, and the bronze coins already mentioned. These provide extremely valuable and varied information on the way of life and customs of the local population of the fourth and fifth centuries.

The results obtained at Bratei provoked a chain reaction. Researches made in various places along the Tîrnava Mare basin have led to the identification of numerous settlements of that period. Special significance attaches to the settlement discovered and searched at Sighişoara in the Dealul Viilor zone, where over seventy houses, domestic storages and ceramic workshops have yielded valuable data upon the way of life of the Daco-Roman population of the fourth to seventh centuries. Numerous settlements discovered afterwards in the Mureş basin at Aiud-Rădeşti, Noşlac, Jernut and Tîrgu-Mureş, and in the Someş basin at Cluj-Mănăştur and Sic, complete in a suggestive way the image of the demographic density of the Daco-Roman population of the fourth century in Transylvania.

A very important role in the chronological determination of the inhabitancy in the Someş basin is played by the settlements of Taga (Cluj district), where the archaeological material discovered in more than twenty earth houses — ceramics, coins, jewellery etc — proves in a very convincing way that the settlements belonged to the fourth century. The material discovered at Taga is identical with that found in Bratei or Sighişoara as well as in the settlements along the lower basin of the Olt River at Hărman, Cernatu and Arcuş, another area which had a large population in the fourth century.

In these settlements, which were in fact real villages, the population lived, as in other areas of Europe, in houses half buried in earth, provided with heating installations. A house of this type may be seen in the village museum at Bucharest, proof that they existed until comparatively modern times. Among other things, the women dealt with spinning and weaving, as is attested by the weaving looms discovered in almost all settlements. The bones of wild animals prove the practice of hunting. But the most important economic activity is undoubtedly represented by agriculture and animal-breeding, suggested by the agricultural tools, carbonized seeds and bones of domestic animals discovered.

An important role in the economic activity of that time was played by ceramic products. In all settlements researchers have discovered a large quantity of ceramics of special quality, the roots of which must be sought in both Roman and Dacian ceramics. In all settlements researchers have discovered a large quantity of ceramics of special quality. Ceramics of the fourth century were produced in local workshops as is shown by the ovens of Sighişoara, Cluj-Napoca, Christeşti and Medieşu Aurit, all in Transylvania, and in Locusteni in Oltenia. The construction of these ovens was similar to that of the Roman epoch, attesting in this way the continuation of some traditions from the time of the Roman province. The perpetuation of Roman traditions can also be seen in Moldavia and Wallachia during the whole of the fourth century. But the ceramic tradition of the free Dacians of the third century is most powerful in Transylvania, where it is found also in a corner of south-eastern Transylvania containing Hărman, Sfîntu Gheorghe etc.

The analyses of burial rites and rituals have brought valuable information about specific customs of the original (or primitive, if that word is preferred) population of the fourth century. In the inhabited areas in the neighbourhood of big Roman towns the traditions of the former province were the more powerful. This is attested by the burial cemeteries of Cluj-Napoca, Alba Iulia, Sarmizegetusa, Turda etc. But in the rural milieu the Dacian element was the more powerful, the population practising even during the fourth century in addition to inhumation — the graves of Suatu (Cluj district), Tirmăvioara (Sibiu district) — the rite of cremation, the burned bones of the dead being placed in simple graves or urns. Researchers have found such cemeteries at Baciu (Someş basin), Cuci (Mureş basin), Sfîntu Gheorghe (the basin of the Olt) and Bratei (Tîrnava basin).

During the fourth century the eastern and southeastern parts of Romania were penetrated by an ethnic mixture led by the Goths. Famous historians have demonstrated in a very convincing manner that the different names of the Goths (Gothonians-Tervingians-Greutungians-Visigoths-Ostrogoths) represented in fact periods of the migration, accompanied by the manifestations of blended cultures in the places of immigration. In this large and diversified process the role of the Daco-Roman population from Moldavia and Wallachia is given special importance.

The archaeological expression of this phenomenon of European importance is represented by the culture of Sîntana de Mureş, Cearneahov, attributed at a certain stage of research to the Goths. Careful analysis made later of the finds from the settlements and cemeteries of this culture showed that, in fact, under an apparent cultural unity there were many local aspects, among which several may be attributed to the original population of Moldavia and Wallachia. It is sufficient to remember the graves of people cremated according to the Dacian tradition, which makes evident the major role the local population played in the blending of the cultures of this period.

Observations based on a study of the chronology of the invasion and the spread of the Sîntana de Mureş culture make obvious the fact that the migration of the Goths altered only to a small extent some areas of Moldavia and Wallachia, mainly those towards the Danube. It may be said that Oltenia was not affected by the migration, and in Transylvania research shows a penetration of the Goths only in the second half of the fourth century, the influence of the migration having minor importance in the archaeological spectrum of the former territory of Dacia Superior. The few cemeteries discovered at Sîntana de Mureș (Mureș district), Palatca (Cluj district) and Vermeș (Bistrița-Năsăud district) are significant in this respect.

Even in the period of the short-lived presence of the Goths in some areas of the north Danubian territory, connections with the Romans were not interrupted. The bridge built by Constantine the Great at Sucidava (Celei) and the chain of fortresses along the Danube in Oltenia or Dobrudja represented real focuses of Romanization in the north Danubian territory. The close connections with the Empire, whose juridical frame is represented by the treaty of 332 concluded by Constantine the Great with the Goths, is suggested in a spectacular way by the wide circulation of Roman bronze coins in Moldavia as well as in Wallachia, but especially in Oltenia, Banat and Transylvania. A happening of major importance in the history of the Goths took place in that period. Because of the strong influence of the Roman imperial civilization in the north of the Danube, and of the major influence of the Romanized local population in the areas where the Goths had settled, the process of Romanization of Gothic society started : in ended centuries later in the south of France, in Spain and in Italy. This fact is indicated by an inscription on a collar in the Pietroasa treasure, Gutan Iowi Hailag, which means "The Goths, St. Jupiter", and the word *rex* — king, unknown until that date to Gothic society — on one of the imitated medallions of the Șimleul-Silvaniei treasure.

At the end of the fourth century and the beginning of the fifth, historical and archaeological sources record at the lower and middle Danube the appearance of a new migratory wave : the invasion of the ethnic mixture led by the Huns. This happening, which caused very difficult problems for the Empire, the stability of the Danube area being kept only by payment of heavy annual tributes, is attested on Romania's territory only in east Moldavia and then along the Danube by isolated discoveries : bronze kettles, diadems, mirrors etc. From the archaeological point of view, the migration of the Huns was accompanied by a certain diminishing of archaeological remains of that period, caused probably by the withdrawal of the local population to more protected zones. This phenomenon did not apply only to Romanian territory ; it was a general phenomenon, recorded also in other areas of Europe. But even in this period of fewer archaeological discoveries, in Transylvania, as well as in the southern and eastern parts of the Carpathians, several settlements can be identified, dating either from the end of the fourth century and the first half of the fifth century, or of the second half of the fifth century. In this respect the complexes of Bratei and Sighişoara in the valley of the Tîrnava Mare River are very significant. Careful observations have established, by means of specific pieces of jewellery of the fifth century, the continuation of the inhabitancy of the area in that period. This also happened in the Mureş basin at Soporul de Cîmpie or in Wallachia at Ploieşti, Cirenşanu and Buduseasca, and in Moldavia at Costisa-Neamţ.

On the other hand, it is obvious that archaeological remains specific to the sixth century, the Ipoteşti-Cîndeşti culture, attested mainly in Wallachia, Oltenia and Moldavia, had its genetic roots in the second half of the fifth century.

The collapse of the supremacy of the Huns in the Battle of Nedao (453) was followed in the Pannonian plain by the domination of a western branch of the Goths known as Gepidae. The central point of this domination was consistently placed in the area of the middle and lower Tisa river. The discovery of tens and hundreds of graves in cemeteries belonging to this people of Germanic origin of the last decades of the fifth century and then of the sixth century is significant in this respect.

Although Jordanes in his work *Getica* estimates that the Gepidae were in possession of the whole of Dacia, archaeological information is far from confirming that this was so. Intensive investigation undertaken in Oltenia has not identified so far a Gepidic presence in the former Lower Dacia. However, in Transylvania, at Moreşti, Cipău, Cluj-Cordoş and Fundătura, researchers have discovered a Gepidic penetration at the end of the fifth century. But as compared to the situation in the Tisa plain, the penetration of the Gepidae in Transylvania was not as marked as it was there. In fact, the Gepidae were involved with Transylvania only by virtue of a treaty signed with the Empire and in its name. There was a similar situation in Gallia, where the Frankish King Childerich acted also by virtue of a treaty concluded with the Empire, in whose name he controlled the given territory. Behind these alliances with barbarian kings one may see the extension of the policy of the imperial Court from Constantinople of not giving up those territories which were considered to belong to the Empire. Is not this the best explanation of the lack of written information concerning the theory of the "complete abandonment" of Dacia ? In the light of such considerations, the similarity of certain pieces from Childerich's grave and those from the first princely grave in Apahida in Cluj county is capable of a rigorous historical interpretation. Thus the golden fibula (brooch) with onion-shaped buttons from Childerich's grave and the one from the Apahida grave are identical. This was a costume piece reserved for high imperial officials and suggests close political relations between Childerich and Omharus, who was buried at Apahida, on the one hand, and with the Empire on the other. The same interpretation must be given, and has been given, to both seal rings found in the graves of the two barbarian chiefs, who thus presented themselves to the Roman populations of Gallia and Transylvania as high officials of the Roman Empire.

The lack of information referring to the original population was one of the major arguments of the supporters of the migrationist theory of Robert Roesler who deny the continuity of the original elements on the territory of Dacia. Another argument used by Roesler is a linguistic one. According to him, the lack of old German elements in the Romanian language could be explained only by a late immigration of the Romanian people from the south of the Danube.

An analysis of the nature of the barbarian domination in general, and of the Gepidic domination in particular, shows in its true light the reason for this lack of Germanic elements. The Gepidic domination in Transylvania was quite short, representing about eighty years of effective presence of the Gepidae in this region. After 568 the Gepidae appear as agents of the Avar domination, from which they borrowed a series of elements of their spiritual and material culture, the influence of the Avar culture being a strong one. But even in those eighty years of effective presence of the Gepidic culture in its most "pure" form, we must take into consideration the following circumstances resulting from an analysis of the political events of those years. A single tendency marks the expansionist policy of the Gepidae: the conquering and keeping of the town of Sirmuim — the gate to Constantinople in the middle Danube region. The centre of the Gepidae was situated in the region included by the Rivers Tisa, Criş and Mureş and the western mountains. The majority of the population settled here, while in Transylvania the Gepidae settled only in a few towns placed especially along the Mureş river, presenting themselves as a superimposed stratum.

Accordingly, the short period of the presence in Transylvania of the Gepidic culture, unaltered by other elements, as well as the small number of the Gepidae who exercised in Transylvania the authority of the Gepidic kingdom, could not generate an influence strong enough to be reflected in the vocabulary of the people or in other parts on the material and spiritual life of the original population.

The decisive argument that confirms the presence of the original population in general is offered by the results of archaeological research.

One of the most outstanding pieces of evidence pointing to the continuity of the original population of Transylvania is provided by ceramics. An analysis of the ceramics of that epoch in Transylvania emphasizes the existence of two completely different groups. The first group, the larger one, belonged to the original Daco-Roman population, and the second to the Gepidae. Ceramics of the first group were made with a certain type of fine grey clay and in their manufacture, as well as in their ornamentation, show similarities to the former epoch as well as to the contemporary ceramics of Wallachia or Oltenia. These ceramics made of fine grey clay, examples of which are in the Brukenthal Museum in Sibiu, were found in Transylvania in the cultural area of Sîntana de Mureş, as well as in some towns (Cluj, Sopor, Sebeş etc) which were not contaminated by elements of the culture of the Gepidae as reflected by their ceramics.

The ceramics of the first group in Transylvania have some elements in common with the so-called Ipoteşti-Cîndeşti culture, which is that of the original Daco-Roman population in Wallachia and Oltenia. A specific feature of this cultural complex is the brown colour of the ceramics in contrast to the grey colour which prevailed in Transylvania. However, in Transylvania and in Wallachia-Oltenia, many ornamental motives were shared. These consist of straight lines, or straight lines with waves, cut in the vessel. In this respect, the similarity of the ornamental motive from a vessel found at Mugeni (end of the third to the beginning of the fourth century) and a ceramic fragment from Brateiu (end of the fifth, first half of the sixth century) is noticeable. The keepers of this tradition of a certain type of ornamentation in ceramics could only have been the original Daco-Roman element of the population.

Another common element of the two cultural areas is represented by rushlights, such as those found at Brateşti (Brazi), Budureasca and Bucharest (Soldier Chivan Street) similar to those of Brateiu.

These similarities between the two cultural areas, Brateiu-Moreşti in Transylvania and Ipoteşti-Cîndeşti beyond the mountains, prove again the existence of the original elements of the population in Transylvania as well as in Wallachia.

The fact that the ceramics of the first group (in Transylvania) belonged to the original population is proved also by another argument. In contrast to the Gepidic ceramics, those of the first group do not represent an isolated phenomenon in the ceramics of the Romanian territory of the first millennium AD. The ceramics of the first group are a link in the chain of the evolutionary process of ceramics of that millennium. In addition to the connections with the ceramics of the previous epoch, ceramics of the first group in Transylvania have a series of elements which link them with the ceramics of the so-called Dridu culture which presented itself in the ninth and tenth centuries in fully crystallized forms and represents the oldest Romanian culture.

In the Dridu culture archaeologists have noticed a type of ceramic made from fine grey clay which has many similarities to the fine grey ceramics of Brateiu and Moreşti. The analogies established between the Brateiu-Moreşti ceramics and the fine grey ceramics of the Dridu culture are represented in vessels of globular form with a well-articulated brim and with a thickened rim-vessels which represent the late but almost identical link with the vessels of Moreşti. Almost all the ornamental motives of the ceramics of the first group of Brateiu or of Moreşti are found again in the pottery of the Dridu culture. The ornamentation in the inside brim or rim of the vessels found at Brateiu or Porumbenii Mici appears also on certain vessels of the Dridu culture.

In contrast to the ceramics of the first group, the ceramics of the second, those of the Gepidae, make an isolated and ephemeral appearance without links with the older epoch and without leaving anything to the later epoch.

Another pointer to the continuation of the Daco-Roman population's existence is the bronze earring with a massive polyhedron — formed cube — a polyhedron is "a solid figure or body bounded by plane faces, especially more than six". This type of earring has also been found in Slovenia at Bled and Krainburg and is attributed to the Roman population. Such bronze earrings with a polyhedron-formed cube have also been found in Transylvania at Cluj-Cordos and at Sighişoara. By analogy with the situation in Slovenia, these earrings also belonged to the original population.

A valuable help in finding material traces which belonged to the original population is offered by the analogies which can be established between the archaeological material of Transylvania and that around Lake Balaton in Hungary on the site of the old settlement named Morgentiana (today Keszthelyfenek) where until the sixth and seventh centuries a Roman population persisted under the domination of the Avars, a nomadic people from central Asia. At Keszthelyfenek researchers have found in the cemetery earrings with small bronze or silver baskets, hairpins of different sizes beautifully decorated (stylus) and bracelets with snake heads, considered typical of the original inhabitants.

Linked to the cemetery of Keszthelyfenek is the cemetery of Bled in Slovenia, where researchers have also discovered hairpins or earrings with small baskets attached to them. In addition, the cemetery at Bled has links with a series of cemeteries in south Bavaria and north Italy which contain objects of a similar kind and belonged to a Roman population which inhabited the area to the springs of the Rhine and of the Rhône. Consequently, one has here a culture formed of certain Roman elements, mostly preserved at Keszthelyfenek, which has, among other things, the hairpin (stylusnädel) as a common element. Such hairpins found in the settlement of Moreşti confirm the presence of the original element of the population in this settlement.

However, one cannot exclude the possibility that a series of pieces, considered as being of Gepidic or Avar origin, might have been worn by the first inhabitants, reflecting in this way the influence these dominant strata of the population exercised, either directly (by the Gepidae) or indirectly (by the Avars).

Thus it results from the findings of archaeology that the presence of the original Daco-Roman population is attested at the end of the fifth century to the beginning of the seventh century by an element of the utmost importance in any material culture: ceramics. Also, in the present stage of research, we can establish some analogies with other Roman groups, especially by the bronze earrings with polyhedron-formed buttons or cubes and by hairpins. These results of archaeological research allow us to indicate precisely the settlements and cemeteries which can be attributed to the original population.

One of the most important and, at the same time, early original settlements is the one at Brateiu, with a rich lits of ceramics and semi-earth huts with stone cutters.

The tools found in this settlement belonged to the original population and prove the prosperous economic life of the people inhabiting the border of the Tîrnava river. One can state on the basis of the ceramics found there that the settlement with semi-earth huts and stone-cutters at Cipău-Sfîntu Gheorghe belonged also to the original population. The kind of dwelling identified in both settlements has similarities in the cultural area Ipotești-Cîndești and appeared especially in the eastern part of this cultural complex. Dwellings of this type have also been identified in the Dridu culture.

The original inhabitants lived also in earth huts without stonecutters in the settlements of Florești, Cipău, Vidrasău, Luduș and Soporul de Cîmpie. Beyond the mountains, this type of dwelling is attested in only one area, at Bozieni.

The presence of the original inhabitants in these settlements is indicated not only by the type of dwelling but also by the ceramics found in the earth huts. The presence also of the original element of the population in the settlements of Morești and Porumbenii Mici is proved by the grey clay ceramics specific to the original population.

At Morești, the archaeological inventory compiled there is another indication of how both populations lived together. At Porumbenii Mici researchers have found at least a presence of the original population, if not a settlement of the original type. More difficult to decide is the presence of the remains of the original element of the population in the cemeteries of this epoch. Some of the cemeteries considered as being Gepidic may belong to the original population. In the cemetery of the village of Hula in Moreşti commune elements of the original population have been buried. These lived in the settlements of Podei, proved by the graves with iron brooches, bronze earrings with polyhedron-shaped buttons etc.

Another reason for accepting the continuity of the original population in the Carpathian-Danubian area is Christianity of the Orthodox rite, embraced by the Daco-Romans from the north of the Danube. If written sources do not give us exact information about north Danubian Christianity, the evidence for the new religion is found in the Christian terminology of the Romanian language as well as in the old Christian monuments and objects found on Romanian territory.

The most recent research indicates that the spread of Christianity in the northern part of the Danube did not happen as a result of activity by official missionaries, as, for example, Nicitas of Remesiana, but as a result of direct contact with the Christian population of the Empire.

Christianity penetrated the former province only in the fourth century, after the recognition of the Christian religion by the Edict of Milan (313) as a free religion which would be supported by the emperors. The spread of Christianity to the north of the Danube in the fourth century is reflected by the Latin origin of most of the Christian terms in the Romanian language. Study of Christian terms proves that they could only have been taken over in the Romanian language before the end of the sixth century because when the Slavs settled in the Empire the links with south-Danubian Latinity were broken.

The Christian terms of Latin origin are the basic ones which refer to the "Christian notions essential and familiar to the people", while the words which came by the Slav-Byzantine channel express only notions of special subjects that were assimilated in an epoch later than that in which the old Daco-Roman Church was organized.

There is a document of the fourth century which indicates the existence of Christian communities in the north of the Danube, more precisely in Oltenia. It is the Novella XI of the Emperor Justinian by which he reorganized the ecclesiastical administration of the Illyricum province after the loss by the Empire of the provinces of Novicum, Pannonia and Dalmatia.

The new archiepiscopate of Justiniana Prima included
also the regions to the north of the Danube, shown in
an excerpt of the Novella XI which says : "This is to
certify that our Republic extended by the will of God
so that it includes also our fortresses on both sides of
the Danube and Viminacium as well as Recidava or Lite-
rata which are over the Danube to be submitted to our
Domination." Consequently the jurisdiction of the Arch-
bishop of Justiniana Prima extended also to south of the
Danube, irrespective of the place where Recidava may
have been located.

In Sucidava in Oltenia (Celei) research has uncovered
the oldest Christian basilica on Romanian territory, and
the Christian community to which the church belonged
was, of course, under the authority of the Bishop of
Agnae who belonged to the diocese of Justiniana Prima.

Information relating to the Christianity of the original population of Transylvania is poorer. There is no
written information which could prove, at least indirectly,
as in Oltenia, the Christianity of the Daco-Roman
population. The researches referring to the period
of the old church of Densus, near Hateg, are so
far only of a hypothetical nature. This church, built of
materials taken from the Roman settlements in the
surroundings, has been constructed in a most peculiar
style. It is square-shaped, and above the cupola supported on walls there rises a tower shaped like a *frustum* of a pyramid. The roof consists of large slabs arranged in steps. Because of this, early Christian monuments
play a decisive role in the illustration of the Christian
religion of the fourth to sixth century in Transylvania.

The early Christian materials of Transylvania are of
several types : rushlights (Alba Iulia, Sarmizegetusa,
Apulum, Dej, Turda), the *donarium* of Biertan, Roman
funeral monuments on which the mourners later engraved
a cross, a Christian monogram (Zlatna, Cluj) and finally
Roman stone art objects showing the scene of the
"Good Shepherd" (Transylvania, Turda). Most of these
objects belong to the fourth century. A single early
Christian collection of objects is dated in the fifth and
sixth centuries: the rushlights of Dej.

This small number of early Christian monuments or
objects expresses a real situation which existed in Dacia
between 270 and 375. The connections with south of the
Danube had not been broken but, in contrast with other
provinces (Dalmatia, Moesia, Pannonia), they were much

weaker. On the other hand, these monuments reflected the religious orientation of the original inhabitants until the arrival of the Huns. The objects we have discussed were originally either from Italy or Africa or from the nearer Latin-speaking provinces — Illyricum or Pannonia (the *donarium* of Biertan, the two Christian stone objects).

After the invasion of the Huns these Latin connections were broken and the Romanian regions entered the sphere of Byzantine influence. This new orientation is proved by the Christian lamp of Dej and the non-Christian rushlight of Partos. As to the ethnic origin of these early Christian monuments and objects, there are several reasons for believing that they belonged to the original population.

The barbarian populations, especially the Goths, would be Christianized in a body only after they had passed over to the Empire. Add to this the fact that these early Christian monuments and objects were found in a region where the Roman provincial economic life was strongest, either in the former urban centres such as Napoca, Potaissa, Apulum or Ampelum or in the former rural settlements such as Biertan.

Hence Christianity began to spread in the former province in the fourth century, as is proved by the Christian terminology of Latin origin as well as by the early Christian monuments. This spread of a new faith was made by the natural contact of peoples on both sides of the Danube and not through a missionary or preacher. The new faith was superimposed on the older pagan faith which, in a sense, was still maintained. In this way, the names of pagan feasts such as Rosalia (Pentecost) and Florilia (Palm Sunday) were maintained with all the customs connected with them.

The Christian terminology of Latin origin concerning the fundamental notions of faith and the religious life is eloquent proof of the Christianization of the largest part of the Daco-Roman population in the fifth and sixth centuries.

The penetration and settlement of the Slavs on the territory of Romania in the sixth century must be regarded in a different way for each region. In Moldavia, Wallachia and Oltenia, one can find the presence of Slavs beginning with the middle of the sixth century, a presence proved archaeologically. After the beginning of the sixth century, when the cemetery of Sărata-Monteoru

was finished, we do not find any Slav culture in Wallachia or Oltenia. It seems that the majority of the Slavs
poured into the Empire, and those who were left were
assimilated by the original Daco-Roman population.

As for Transylvania, we cannot speak about a penetration of the Slavs until after 680. Even after this date
Slavs did not settle in massive numbers. This is why
the first graves that are purely Slav are in the tumular
cemeteries of Someşeni and Nuşfalău, dated in the eighth
century and the beginning of the ninth century. However,
Slav elements of the seventh century have been found in
Transylvania at Bezid, Sălaşuri and Filiaşi.

At the same time, one must emphasize the presence of
the original element of the population or at least the influence exerted by this element, indicated by fragments
of ceramics made with the wheel and of a paste with
gravel or a very good paste with fine sand decorated with
a large band of lines on the shoulder of the vessel. This
feature of the inventory of ceramics is an indication of
the "evident autochthonous-Slav nature of these settlements", in which the local contribution represented eighty
per cent and the Slav contribution the remainder. This
situation is reflected also in the ceramic material from
Filiaşi.

The rarity of Slav material in Transylvania corres-
pons to the real situation of the sixth and seventh
centuries. In that period some sporadic Slav elements
penetrated Transylvania, where they were rapidly assimilated by the local population of original stock.

After the seventh century the Gepidic culture disappeared without leaving a perceptible trace in the culture
of this region in the following epochs, but elements of
the original culture were represented as one of the
essential components of the Dridu culture.

At the end of the sixth century and the beginning of
the seventh elements of a Slavonic type appeared in the
culture of Transylvania but these were rapidly assimilated by the culture of the original inhabitants into whom
the Slavs were incorporated. A process similar to that of
Transylvania was represented in the south and east of
the Carpathians by the Ipoteşti-Cîndeşti culture. Here too
the Slav elements, inserted among the original elements
of the population, were to disappear in a final stage,
the culture thus regaining its unity and forming another
essential component of the Dridu culture, the oldest in
Romania. In the eighth to tenth centuries these two

cultural components, the carriers of which were the Daco-Roman inhabitants of Wallachia, Oltenia and Transylvania, joined together with other elements in the Dridu culture.

In her booklet *Eastern Romanity until the First Romanian Political Units*, the archaeologist Ligia Bârzu said that the Bratei culture, dated chiefly to the fifth and sixth centuries, was known in several settlements, such as Obreja, Sighişoara and Moreşti. Naturally, if compared with the contents of Cemetery 1 at Bratei, there were later changes, such as the almost complete disappearance of the red pottery, a prevalence of earthenware made of a coarse-grained grey clay thrown on the fast wheel, a narrower range of shapes, a considerable drop in imports. Despite this poor display, the Roman mark was not lost. The major proof was in the coarse-grained grey clay ceramics which, for all their inherent changes, evinced obvious Roman traditions in both technique and range of forms. Highly characteristic was the conservation of the storage vessel, so very specific for the Dacian provincial pottery, and of the pitcher with a trefoil-shaped mouth also made by hand at Bratei and found in a pithouse dated to the sixth and seventh centuries.

Characteristic of the Transylvanian variant of the culture revealed by the contents of Cemetery 1 at Bratei is the prevalence of the fast-wheel-thrown grey pottery and the very low percentage of hand-made pottery. The last detail was, in Mrs Bărzu's opinion, important for indicating the time when the groups of late Dacians were integrated into the Daco-Roman community.

This was the material culture which the Gepidae found on their settling down in Transylvania. It was a well-established culture which they could not significantly alter or influence. The only elements ascribable to the Gepidae were the several fibulae with plate and the vessels or fragments of stamped or glossy pottery.

The Costişa-Botoşana cultural aspect probably developed against the Bîrlad-Valea Seacă background in eastern Moldavia. Here again the perpetuation of shapes of Roman vessels was obvious with the wheel-thrown grey pottery, but so far as the technique was concerned, the set-back was readily perceivable. This set-back concerned the gradual replacement of the fast with the slow wheel which, by the end of the sixth century, was complete. Then, unlike in Transylvania, there was a larger proportion of hand-made pottery of Dacian tradition. This was explainable by the different degree of Romanization of the two regions, by the endurance of traditional Dacian culture and its particular forms in the fourth century and the first part of the fifth. In Romania's east Carpathian regions, the Costişa-Botoşana culture is that of the original stock which incorporated and assimilated the Slavic ethnic and cultural elements.

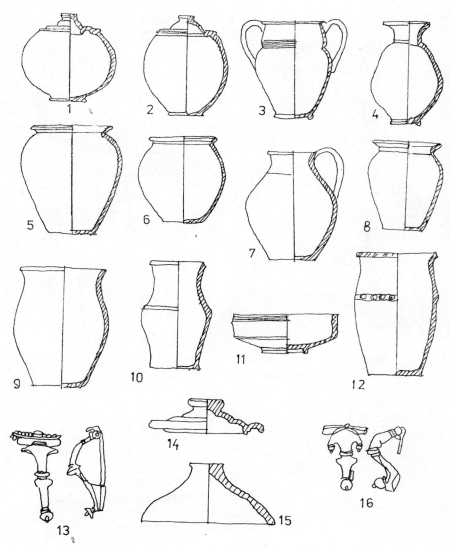

Dacian continuity in Roman Dacia (cemetery from the 2nd-3rd centuries AD at Soporul de Cîmpie, Cluj county). 1-8, 11, 14, 15 wheelmade pottery modelled in red or grey paste ; 9, 10, 12 hand-made pottery; 13, 16 fibulae.

Culture of the Romanized population in Transylvania in the 4th-6th centuries (Bratei culture 1). 1,3-5,9 wheel-made pottery ; 2 earring ; 6-8 fibulae.

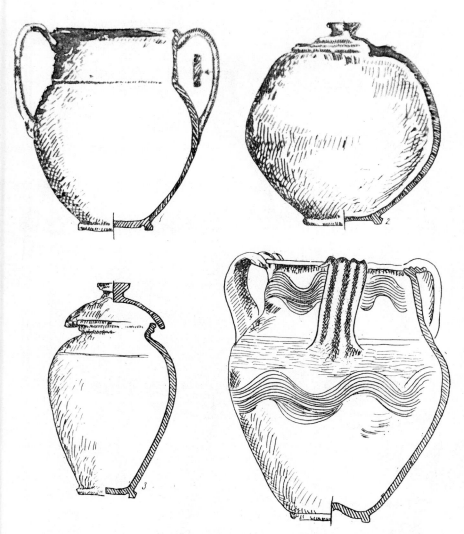

Roman Funeral urns from the cemetery of Soporul de Cîmpie (Second and third centuries, AD).

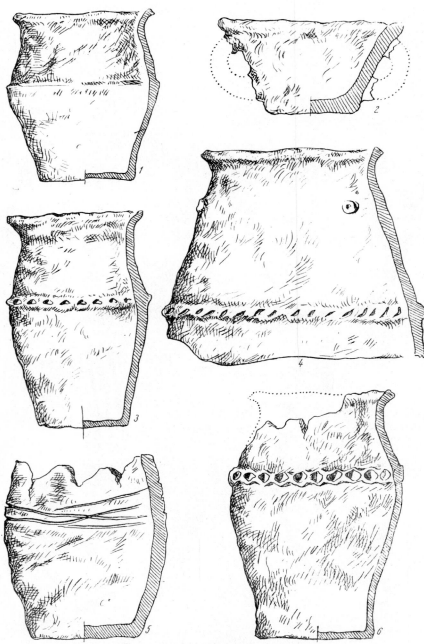

Dacian hand-made ceramics buried at Soporul de Cîmpie.

11. The Great Debate

An attempt to specify in Romanian history a chronological limit between late antiquity and the Middle Ages must take into consideration the specific conditions of all the former territories of the Roman Empire. This limit was not a rigid one and was not everywhere the same but was placed in a historical process of continually changing circumstances of material life and socio-political relations. For the south and south-east regions of Romania one has the tendency to place the beginning of the Middle Ages at the start of the seventh century, when the Roman-Byzantine boundary along the Danube collapsed and the Slavs of the first wave of their migration settled permanently in the Balkan Peninsula.

However, the partitioning of the history of a people cannot rely only upon the events of political history or of external circumstances but must take into account, first of all, the internal evolution of that society. From this point of view, as has already been stated, the period between the fourth and the seventh centuries AD meant, for Daco-Roman society, continuous changes and gradual ethnic evolution. The process took place over a very large area, from the northern Carpathians to the Balkans, on both sides of the Danube, with different intensities, different speeds and even different centres of change from one epoch to another. Most opinions expressed in Romanian and foreign specialized literature place in the eighth century the time when one can speak of a Romanic people, the Romanian people, in this part of the Continent, descended from the Eastern Roman world and individualized by language and civilization in comparison with the other neo-Latin peoples of Europe.

From an archaeological point of view, this chronological limit is justified by the discoveries confirming the

beginnings in that century of the manifestations of the
Dridu culture, which characterized, until the ninth century, the old Romanian rural communities. The acceptance
of this internal limit is also supported by Eastern, Byzantine and Central European written sources, which mention the Romanians as representing a distinctive ethnic
group in the ninth century and at the beginning of the
tenth century.

The ending of the formation of the Romanian people
in the eighth century took place under conditions of the
presence in the lower Danube area of the first Slav
migratory waves and of their partial assimilation by the
Romanic population. In the larger context of political
history in Eastern Europe, the end of the eighth century
meant the collapse of the power and domination of the
Avars under the concentrated blows of the Carolingian
Empire and of the first Bulgar tsardom and the creation
of favourable conditions for the formation of the inci-
pient feudal structures of local society. The formation in
the first half of the ninth century of the Great Moravian
principality of the western Slavs coincided with the first
Romanian political structures coming to maturity in the
eastern part of the Carpathian basin in the same century. They are mentioned as "duchies" by AD 900 by
the oldest Hungarian chronicles, when the installation by
896 of the Hungarian tribes in Pannonia (present-day
Hungary) caused the first confrontation between the
newcomers and the local population. The Hungarians
were a people of Finno-Ugric origin who, led by and
mixed with Turkic groups, came from the steppes north
of the Black Sea, being driven from there by the
Pechenegs. For a short time during the ninth century
they resided in the so-called Atelkuz ("between rivers") in
the eastern part of Dacia and skirted it to the north, as
archaeological finds have clearly proved.

As is pointed out in the *Concise History of Romania,*
the Hungarian military raids in the north-west and west
of the Transylvanian plateau during the first half of the
tenth century, after having wiped out the Moravian
principality and the proto-Bulgar controlled political organizations in Crisana and Banat, created a new situation
in these regions which was to terminate after 1001 with
the gradual conquest of Transylvania and the implanting
there of foreign colonies. The Magyars took little time to
assimilate the Slavs they had found in the plains of the

central part of their new homeland, and the political predominance of the Slavs on the Transylvanian plateau also came to an end at this time.

In close connection with this situation is the wide expansion, attested in the early years of the century, of the native population, bearers of the Dridu culture. On the Transylvanian plateau this culture reached the line of the Mureș (Blandiana, Sebeș etc). The fact that the oldest material culture of the people in Maramureș — archaeologically identified as thirteenth-century Siliș-tea Veche and in the Romanian village of Sărăsău on the Tisa, and continued in the culture of the fourteenth century princely villages of Dragoș and Bogdan, for example, at Cuhea — obviously originated in the Transylvanian culture of the eighth and ninth centuries and in the Dridu culture, is confirmation that the Romanians had been in Maramureș for centuries and that the cultures just mentioned were really Romanian.

In the extra-Carpathian regions the Pechenegs, a new group of nomadic and warlike Asian herdsmen who had come from beyond the Volga and the Urals as a first echelon of a larger group that was to include the Udi and the Cumans, put an end to proto-Bulgar domination and for the first time created conditions that resulted in the decline of the political power of the Slavs. In the tenth century, as previously on similar occasions, no destruction or expulsion of the native population over wide areas is attested. The demographic expansion of the population in the same century is proved throughout Moldavia. Even the native settlements in the territories east of the River Siret in Moldavia continued to exist until the first half of the eleventh century, as proved by the Byzantine bronze coins found there. It was only around 1027 that the Pechenegs were to take their flocks and herds and their warlike horsemen to the plains of Romania on the occasion of their first independent raid into the Byzantine Empire.

It is not improbable that the Byzantine Empire endeavoured to forestall the Magyar threat, as suggested by the Byzantine stone strongholds built at Slon in the Buzău Mountains immediately after 971. Byzantine coins which had again begun to infiltrate north of the Danube and even up to upper Moldavia in the early years of the tenth century now reached extra-Carpathian Dacia in large numbers, as did also Byzantine craftware and other goods. A rapid development of the settlements of the native population has been ascertained. These developments and the domestic happenings accompanying them in Dacia marked the final stage of the ethnogenetic process which also showed a tendency towards maximum extension over the territory of ancient Dacia. The mention made of the Vlachs (Romanians) in the Balkans by a Byzantine source of the eleventh century referring to developments in 976, and the fact that such remarks subsequently increased in number, is of outstanding significance when compared with the mentions made from the eighth to the eleventh century on the Romanian population north of the Danube, designated as Blasi in the chronicle of the anonymous notary of King Béla III (generally referred to by historians as "Anonymous"), early tenth century, Volohi in the old Russian chronicle (late ninth century), and the country Balak in the Armenian geography (eighth and ninth centuries). As Vlach was the name then given by the Germans and Slavs to the Romanic peoples, the last two mentions cited above cannot be used to establish the moment when Romanian ethnogenesis ended. The final moment of that process might be considered to be the time when the last Slav groups were assimilated. It should be noted that Vlach was the name given to the Romanians by other peoples in the Middle Ages, though the Romanians themselves have always called themselves Romanians.

The Romanian duchies or *voivode*-ships covered the entire Romanian intra-Carpathian territory. In the Bihor region, which corresponds to the north-western regions of Romania, bounded by the Mureş and Someş rivers and stretching from the peaks of the western Carpathians to the Tisa river, the territory was ruled in those years by the *voivode* Menumorut. The political and military centre of Bihor region was in the Biharia fortress, not far from Oradea, where there still remains an impressive fortification of earth and wood which has been searched with convincing archaeological results. Most significant is the mention of the main source of the events that followed in *Gesta Hungarorum*, compiled by Anonymous towards the close of the twelfth century on the basis of written records which have been lost and of oral tradition. However, *Gesta Hungarorum* still exists in a museum in Vienna. In this chronicle Menumorut was considered both a local ruler and the *protégé* of the Byzantine emperor of Constantinople. This feeling of belonging to the Empire, initially to the Roman and then to the Byzantine Empire, represented a constant element during the first millennium AD for the Romanized and Christianized population left outside the political and military boundaries of the Empire for shorter or longer periods.

Narrating the evolution of the events, Anonymous's chronicle reports the attack and the conquest by the Hungarian cavalry of the Satu Mare fortress, which is placed on the Someş river, not far from the point where the Someş river meets the Tisa river. After the negotiations which failed because of the refusal of the *voivode* of Satu Mare to give up land to the newcomers, the Hungarians went to Biharia fortress, which they conquered. The story of how the *voivode* of Bihor could have retired to the mountains, where he could have arrived at an agreement with the supreme chief of the Hungarian tribes by a well-known solution used in the Middle Ages, namely the marriage between a son and a daughter of the opposing leaders, reflects most probably two historical distinct and parallel realities. On the one hand, during the tenth century the *voivode*-ship of Bihor continued to exist under the military control of the Hungarians in the course of their settlement of the area. It was only by the middle of the next century that the integration of the region in the kingdom founded by Arpad's followers took place during the foundation of the Oradea bishopric and later of Bihor county. On the other hand, in Bihor, as well as in other regions of Romania, the military pressure and the threat of the migratory waves caused a certain territorial reorganization of the local inhabitans, concentration of settlements in more sheltered zones and even the temporary abandonment of some villages in open areas and on the main routes of the migratory tribes. At the end of the first millennium the density of the population must have been less than three or four inhabitants per square kilometre, but the happenings described did not affect the historical evolution of the social groups or the continuity of life on the larger areas of the country, as we have seen in our study of the settlements in the Olt valley, although there were times when Comana de Jos was abandoned, possibly because of flooding.

By the first years of the tenth century there was another "duchy" in the south-western part of Romania, between the Mureş and Danube rivers, a region which later was to receive the name of Banat. According to some sources, this area was ruled by *voivode* Glad, in whose army Pechenegs and Bulgars fought together with the Romanians. It is possible that during the ninth century, after the fall of the Avars, the first Bulgarian tsardom had taken over the inheritance left by the Avars. Glad's fortresses were placed on the Danube, but the decisive confrontation of his troops with the Hungarian cavalry could have taken place, according to the chronicle, on the Timis river. The battle ended with the defeat of the local forces, and for a short time these regions were ruled by the Hungarians. The effective integration of Banat and, in the beginning, only the area of its plain in the Hungarian feudal kingdom founded in 1000 was realized later, in the first decades of the eleventh century. Meanwhile, the centre of the *voivode*-ship of Banat was removed to the north, on the border of Mureş, at Cenad (Urbs Morisena), where Ahtum, a descendant of *voivode* Glad, ruled and where there was an important monastery with friars of the Church of Constantinople. In the conflict between the *voivode* of Banat and the first crowned king of Hungary, Stephen I, the Hungarian ruler was victorious and Ahtum, betrayed by his friends, was killed. An important treasure containing twenty-three golden vessels, discovered almost two centuries ago at Sînnicolau Mare, near Cenad, and now in the Kunsthistoriches Museum at Vienna, is considered to be a reflection of these events, as it was probably buried during or after the battle.

The third Romanian *voivode*-ship which suffered in the first years of the tenth century as a result of the appearance in the Carpathian basin of the Magyar tribes, extended "beyond the forest" as against the Tisa plain, for which reason it was called Terra Ultra Silvana — Transylvania. This "duchy" stretched on both sides of the middle Someş river to the middle basin of the middle Mureş river and was ruled by the Romanian *voivode* Gelu — *"Gelu quidam Blacus"* (Vlach), as is mentioned in the same Hungarian chronicle. It added that the people of this country was formed of Romanians and Slavs and praised the riches and fertility of Transylvania. After the defeat of the *voivode* of Bihor and after sending spies to make inquiries about Gelu's military force, the Hungarian horsemen penetrated to the gates of Mureş on the territory of the Romanian *voivode* in a rapid campaign which annihilated the resistance to the attack at the border by the classical tactics adopted so many times by the migratory armies from the Eastern steppes. Gelu's army tried to resist on the Almaş river but its inferiority in weapons, which consisted of bows and arrows, as well as the superior military force of the Hungarian cavalry, assured the invader's victory. Trying to retreat towards his fortress near the Someş river, Gelu was caught and killed on the borders of the Căpuş river.

As to the historical circumstances of the Transylvanian *voivode*-ship during the tenth century, the same chronicle tells us that Tuhutum, a Hungarian chief accepted by the inhabitants of Transylvania, ruled over Gelu's country. The "duchy" of 900 continued to exist, with its institutions, but the centre moved to the south at Alba Iulia ("the Transylvanian Alba" — Bălgrad) situated on the Mureş river where, in the second half of the tenth century, research has attested the presence of a princely dynasty which entered into relations with the Church of Constantinople, receiving from it a hierarchy under a bishop. As a result of a campaign organized by King Stephen I of Hungary against the *voivode*-ship of Alba Iulia in 1002 or 1003, the princely dynasty of that place was removed. However, in the following centuries Transylvania continued to be organized as a *voivode*-ship, even though it was dependent on the Hungarian Crown, a *voivode*-ship which was maintained until the sixteenth century, when it became a principality under Turkish suzerainty. This reflected the firm nature of the local institutions at the end of the first millennium AD.

These fragments of military and political history are given a broader and more convincing reflection in recent archaeological discoveries. Thus, in order to know the ethnic-demographical realities of the end of the eighth century and during the ninth century we must take into consideration the hundreds of settlements and cemeteries discovered which attest the impressive uniformity of the cultural and material aspects of life at the time in the whole territory of Romania. In the Romanian intra-Carpathian territory there are numerous cemeteries of the eighth and ninth centuries, called for convenience the "Mediaş-Bratei type", which were bi-ritual, reflecting the conservation until a relatively late epoch of the old practices and faiths within the synthesis of Christianity and that which originated in folk beliefs of the Daco-Roman population before the organization of their own churches with bishops. At the same time, researchers have also discovered cemeteries with tumular graves of cremated bodies (Someşeni, Nuşfalău) belonging to some Slav groups which penetrated the territory of Transylvania in the ninth century after the fall of the Avars. These Slav groups, representing the second Slav migratory wave on Romania's territory, are mentioned in written sources as living together with the Romanians in the territory of Romania.

In the Romanian extra-Carpathian territories stretching to the lower Danube and to the Black Sea, for the same period of the eighth and ninth centuries there are a great many cemeteries in which the remains of Christian and non-Christian elements of the population were buried. Such people lived closer together than those in the Byzantine Christian hierarchical centres. Among these cemeteries there are those recently searched at Izvorul and Frăteşti in the Giurgiu district and at Obîrşia Noua in the Dolj district.

The discoveries of archaeological material of that period and the classification of it in accordance with the area confirm that there were concentrations of population in the valleys of the most important rivers which spring from the Carpathians and flow south to the Danube in settlements around fortifications of earth and wood. These reflect a stage of political organization which marks the development of feudal relations similar to those existing in the same period in Transylvania. These archaeological realities are confirmed by Byzantine sources of the tenth century which attest, on the occasion of the return of the Empire to the Danube, the existence in the Romanian plain of chiefs who ruled over fortresses and were subdued by the Byzantine Emperor John Tzimiskes when he, after a victorious campaign in the north of the Balkan Peninsula, put an end to the first Bulgarian tsardom and consolidated the Byzantine boundaries along the Danube in 971.

At this stage we can look back on the controversies about what happened when the Emperor Aurelian withdrew his legions and the administrative apparatus of that part of the Roman Empire between 271 and 275-6. One school of thought, mainly Hungarian, maintains that the Daco-Roman element of the population was withdrawn with them and another, the Romanian, says that the settlers stayed where they were until the two cultures, Dacian and Roman, gradually merged and the Romanian race was born. The Romanians accept Anonymous's account of what happened when the Magyars entered Transylvania but the Hungarians, apparently, do not, because to do so would be an admission that the country was populated by an organized society.

In his book *Transylvania* (Bucharest, 1983), Lieutenant-General Dr Ilie Ceaușescu, president of the Romanian Commission of Military History, says that "Although *Gesta Hungarorum* records perfectly true data and facts, some Hungarian historians question the authenticity of what King Béla's Anonymous Notary recorded minutely, saying that the parts referring to the Romanians are "fables", "legends" or "fairy tales"; but when the chronicle refers to other historical events, the Anonymous Notary is appreciated as "one of the most distinguished Magyar historians", a "peerless geographer" and "well conversant with historiography". In other words, when he refers to the Romanians he is not to be trusted but in other respects he is to be highly praised.

If the Romanians were not at the places described, who were the builders of the fortresses whose remains have been found in modern times? Migratory tribes? If so, one would expect to find evidence of their culture but such evidence has not been uncovered. Would people in the course of their passage across a country stay long enough in one place to build a fortress, which would imply residence? The indications are that the Magyars were opposed by people who had been long established in Transylvania.

The Romanian historian Dr Nicolae Stoicescu argues in *The Continuity of the Romanian People* (Bucharest, 1983), that a particularly important argument of the advocates of continuity, which has not yet been answered by its adversaries, pertains to the domain of logic, viz : how was it possible that the Romanian people should return after a millennium exactly to the same place which their forefathers had left?

A strong argument in support of the thesis that the Daco-Romans could not have left their ancestral land is the richness of the land. The historian C. C. Giurescu said that :

> The richness of the Carpatho-Danubian land made people live on it from the remotest pre-historical times, from the paleolithic age down to our days. Such a land that supplies abundant and varied food, that contains salt and gold in its entrails, not to

mention the other riches, such a land cannot be abandoned. Therefore only naive or ill-meaning people can imagine that on an order of the emperor from distant Rome, the Daco-Roman peasants left their fields, their houses and all their belongings to cross the Danube, and settle in the much poorer land of Moesia, which in fact was not less menaced than their former country. At home they had all they needed; so they stayed there and paid taxes to another master, the German, Slav or Asian invader who had no reason to kill his subjects because it meant killing those who fed him, his source of income, destroying his own fortune. The richness of the Romanian soil is a guarantee of the Daco-Roman's continuity in Dacia Trajana.

It may be argued that in Dacia the ruling system practised by most invaders was that of indirect domination, the exploitation being carried out through the governing bodies of the native people, the only ones who were obliged to work and produce goods. The invaders were mainly soldiers who were unable to live by themselves, not being tillers of the land, they needed the natives to provide them with the food they could not produce and of which they took only a part.

The geographer Vintilă Mihăilescu asks how was it possible to have a numerous Romanian population in Moldavia and Wallachia, both regions exposed to barbarian invasions, and that such a population should be absent from the natural fortress of Transylvania, well defended by its mountains?

It may also be argued that Transylvania had always constituted a strong reservoir of Romanian populations and that, throughout the Middle Ages, the movements of population followed exactly a direction opposite to that alleged by the adversaries of continuity: not from Wallachia and Moldavia towards Transylvania but from this province to the sister provinces south and east of the Carpathians; Movements of flocks from south of the Danube and the Carpathians to Transylvania have never been recorded: it is a natural impossibility, for Transylvania, lying on the northern and western side of the mountains, has no good pasture lands. For this reason no shepherd from the south would dream of driving his flocks to Transylvania.

It is reasonable to ask what measures could have been employed by the authorities to force the Daco-Roman settlers to leave their farms and settlements and migrate south of the Danube. True, the army could have been used for this purpose, but they themselves were involved in a major move of quarters and probably did not have the time to scour the countryside, often to remote spots, rounding up settlers, whom they would have to accommodate and feed before starting the trek to the south. Peasants have a fierce devotion to their land. If they were threatened with dispossession, all they had to do was hide in the forests or mountains until the soldiers had gone and then return to their land. All in all, the evidence supports R. W. Seton-Watson's view, expressed in his *History of the Roumanians* that, "It is safe to assume that the wealthier settlers withdrew from north of the Danube, but the great mass of the population remained behind."

Seton-Watson also points out that, beginning with the Goths and Gepids, almost all the many peoples who flooded into southern Europe between the third and tenth centuries passed first over Romanian soil. But it is to be noted that in every case the object of invasion lay beyond: the glittering plunder of Byzantium and of the rich Italian cities beckoned the barbarians onward. The Dacia of Trajan was a mere stage on the road, and nothing is more surprising than that the Goths in particular should have left virtually no trace throughout the territory in question. The absence of Gothic words in the Romanian language has sometimes been used to prove the lack of continuity of the Romanian race on the northern bank of the Danube: but to such arguments, admittedly resting upon mere conjecture, it may fairly be replied that if the Daco-Romans had in the fourth century already been concentrated south of the Danube, Gothic influences on their language would have been quite inevitable, in view of the extent to which the Goths established themselves in what we now know as Bulgaria.

Another question is whether it was possible that in a territory of barely tens of thousands of square kilometres like the ancient Roman province of Dardania, from which the Romanians (Vlachs) were alleged to have come, huge masses of people in the range of hundreds of thousands could have been on the move? What triggered off that movement, unprecedented, judging by the area covered and the masses of people involved, in the medieval history of south-east and east Europe? What was the reaction of Constantinople, which had just established its control over the peninsula, in the face of a possible loss of hundreds of thousands of subjects? Also, why was a migration of such magnitude, if it took place, not fully recorded at the time ?

These questions go unanswered.

12. Feudal Dwellings Found

The unitary evolution of the Romanian society on the territories situated on both sides of the Carpathians, attested by identical cultural manifestations and by the fact that they passed through common stages in their historical development, was interrupted in the tenth century by the last migratory waves which affected the Carpathian-Danubian-Pontic area. In a period when western Europe, overcoming the crisis produced by the Arab and Norman invasions and having to suffer only occasionally because of the raids by Magyars, could dedicate itself to its medieval construction, in the east the series of late disturbances inaugurated by the Magyars in 896 was followed by the arrival of the Pechenegs, Udis, Cumans and Huns and in the middle of the thirteenth century by the big invasion of the Mongols (1241). These circumstances of political history caused the slowing down and even the stagnation of Romania's sociopolitical development in certain periods, postponing until the thirteenth and fourteenth centuries the creation of the life of a Romanian state in stable and final forms.

Although written sources attest that the Pechenegs, of Turkish origin, had been present along the lower Danube ever since the tenth century, archaeological discoveries indicate that during the whole of that century rather peaceful living conditions prevailed in settlements that do not show signs of destruction or the effects of crises. It thus appears that the activity of the Pechenegs before 1000 consisted of short raids, the taxation of the local population, and the wielding of a nominal authority from their tribal centres situated east of the territories inhabited by the Romanians.

In these conditions, the return of the Byzantine Empire to the Danube in the last third of the tenth century had a favourable influence on Romanian society situated

north of the Danube. Stability was ensured by the numerous Danubian fortresses and towns which were economic, cultural and religious centres, rebuilt or newly built
by the Byzantines. A search of the settlements of the
plain zone situated east and south of the Carpathians
reveals disorders and changes after 1000, several settlements being abandoned in favour of the Danubian centres protected by the Empire or the regions situated at
the foot of the mountains, where one could find denser
settlements. During the whole of the eleventh and twelfth
centuries Romanian settlements were concentrated in the
more sheltered regions, especially around the Carpathians,
and in the so-called "countries" (from the Latin term
terrae) which represent natural subdivisions of the varied
territories inhabited by the Romanians. Later, in the
thirteenth century, under more favourable conditions of
political history, the unifying action of the Romanian
feudal rulers was to start from these "countries".

In the territories situated east and south of the Carpathians, the events that took place there soon after 1000
were caused by the effective penetration of the Pechenegs. They did not leave traces of their presence in the
form of settlements or of cemeteries in the literal sense
of the words because, being nomads, cattle-breeders and
warriors preoccupied with plundering and with obtain-
ing regular revenues from the local communities, they
were permanently on the move over large distances.
Only recently researches have discovered some solitary
graves of Pecheneg warriors, with contents which belong
to the eleventh century, all in the region of the Danube
plain, where other place-names of Turkish, Pecheneg or
Cuman origin attest the historical role these nomads
played there.

The Cumans, or Polovtsians, as the Slav eastern sources called them, penetrated, after the Pechenegs and the
Udi into the lower Danube at the end of the eleventh
century. By the end of the twelfth century they had
settled in some zones and, as had happened with the Pechenegs a century earlier, they lost their ethnic identity, being assimilated by the local population. The fact
that the Pechenegs lived together with the Romanians in
the south of Transylvania was not mentioned until the
beginning of the thirteenth century, when there was a
reference to "the Romanians' and the Pechenegs' forest"
(Silva Blacorum et Bissenorum). The majority of the Cumans moved west to the Tisa region, when the arrival of

the Mongols, in the third and fourth decades of the thirteenth century, put their dwellings in danger. Entering into the protection of the Hungarian kings, they still played a role for a while in the events of the region before losing their identity among the Hungarian villagers.

In Transylvania and in other Romanian intra-Carpathian territories, the events of political history connected with the arrival of the Hungarian tribes and their gradual spread from west to east caused a concentration of the Romanian settlements in the peripheral zones. Even after the encouragement by the Hungarian kings of the Saxon colonization by the middle of the twelfth century, the Romanian population in the whole of Transylvania maintained itself at around sixty-five to seventy per cent, while in the sheltered zones of the periphery the proportion reached about ninety per cent and even more. Archaeological discoveries and written sources such as chronicles and chancellory documents confirm the presence in these nineteen "countries" from the edge of Transylvania and its mountain zones of a dense and homogeneous Romanian settlement in the eleventh to thirteenth centuries. These "countries", which later became countries or districts in the administrative and political organization imposed by the Hungarian kingdom in the fourteenth and fifteenth centuries, stretched along the Carpathians from the Danube to the springs of the Tisa river over a distance of almost fifteen hundred kilometres if we take into account the Apuseni Mountains. These "countries" included Almaj, Hațeg, Amlaș, Făgăraș, Bîrsa, Năsăud, Lăpuș, Maramureș, Oaș, Codru, Beiuș, Hălmagi and several other territorial structures, including a variable number of village settlements of twenty to twenty-five villages in the smaller "countries", territorial structures which even today keep their own individuality in the type of inhabitant and folk belief.

The homogeneous nature of the society within the naturally defined regions of these "countries" at the beginning of the Middle Ages is reflected in the living-conditions of that epoch. This fact applies to the Carpatho-Danubian territories as well as to many other zones of Europe. The common utilization of the natural resources, the organization of the productive processes which allowed the people to gain a living with the modest technical means of those times, the community institutions which could assure the production and the reproduction of a society on a territory which included tens of village settlements, indicate a cohesion which could have been achieved only by the unitary nature of these territorial structures.

As to the social nature of structures of the "country" type at the beginning of the Romanian Middle Ages, they were, without any doubt, first of all unions of village communities. Their evolution towards the generation of feudal relations by the end of the first millennium AD and the beginning of our millennium has been reconstructed mainly as a result of archaeological research. The pre-feudal beginnings of the Romanian "countries" corresponding to the information about the "duchies" and *voivode*-ships of the ninth and tenth centuries are not too far from the time when the eligible "judges" (the word is derived from the Latin *judex*) and the "old people of the villages" (the first term from *veteranus,* the second from *fossatum*), or the "good old people", ruled the community institutions. Later these territorial structures suffered social differentiations and experienced the deepening of the new feudal relationships.

A series of monuments and archaeological complexes preserved in the Romanian "countries" on both sides of the Carpathians confirms social differentiations which existed before the thirteenth and fourteenth centuries. These are also mentioned in chancellory documents. These discoveries reflect at the same time a certain stage of socio-political organization of society, a stage which can be considered as characteristic of the period which directly preceded the constitution and affirmation of the Romanian medieval states on the political scene of eastern Europe. Recent researches have concentrated mainly on Transylvania but, as will be seen later, similar archaeological findings apply to the Romanian extra-Carpathian territories.

Thus the excavations begun in the 1960s in Maramureş county, a "country" which is identified with the basin of the springs of the Tisa river and which, with its ten thousand square kilometres and over a hundred villages represented one of the largest and most important Romanian pre-statal structures, have resulted in the transition of written sources referring to the political organization of Romanian society before the fourteenth century into concrete material testimonies. The fortified residence of the Bogdan family discovered at Cuhea (today Bogdan Vodă, Maramureş district) on the Isa river, a tributary of the Tisa river, included in its enclosure a big tower-dwelling made of wood on stone foundations which had two stages of construction. The older residence, in the twelfth and thirteenth centuries, was destroyed by fire and was rebuilt in a very similar way, lasting, as a new stage of the complex, until the middle of the fourteenth century, when the building was again destroyed by fire and finally abandoned. This corresponds to the time of departure of Bogdan of Cuhea, *voivode* of Maramureş before 1343, to the north of Moldavia, where by 1359 he became the first independent prince of the Romanian principality east of the Carpathians.

The passage of the Romanian military and political nucleus from the intra- to the extra-Carpathian area in the twelfth to fourteenth centuries was a result of the pressure put by the Hungarian Crown on Romanian society in the boundaries of Transylvania. This was one of the so-called "traditions" mentioned in the chronicles under the name of the "settling-down". The passage of Bogdan and his warriors from Maramureş, to Moldavia by the middle of the fourteenth century was the last of these "settlings-downs". Similar events had taken place earlier from the south of Transylvania to the north of Wallachia and Oltenia on the territory of the future "Romanian country", also known to foreign sources under the name of Wallachia.

At Cuhea (Bogdan Vodă) researchers have also discovered the remains of the Court's church, built of rubble at the beginning of the fourteenth century on the site of an older church made of wood. The cemetery of this church contained jewellery, of the twelfth to fourteenth centuries. These recent researches have put in a new light the problem of the beginnings of medieval architecture which used rubble, including, often, stones from rivers, on the territory of Romania as well as the possible continuation, in some regions, of the stone, brick and rubble civilization of late antiquity to the Middle Ages. On the one hand, in the north and north-east of Romania, in those zones which did not belong to the Roman province of Dacia and where it was supposed that the passage of the peasant architecture of wood to the feudal one of rubble had taken place only in the fourteenth and fifteenth centuries, even later in some zones, researchers have discovered ruins (foundations) of some representative feudal monuments of the twelfth and thirteenth centuries, such as those of Giuleşti (Maramureş district), Bîtca

Doamnei and Tîrgu Neamţ (Moldavia), belonging to the *voivodes* and princes (feudal lords) of the period preceding the complete crystallization of the medieval state.

At the same time, in the central zones of Romania, in the south of Transylvania and in the north of Wallachia, researchers have found the remains of rubble monuments, many of them built of materials used by the Romans and taken from ancient ruins or fitted up by the re-utilization of Roman constructions in the eleventh and twelfth centuries. Among them are the rotunda of the present cathedral at Alba Iulia, the church of Densus, the churches of Streisîngeorgiu and Peşteana, and another four monuments discovered later in Hunedoara district which, in the second and third centuries AD, was also the centre of the Roman province.

Finally, new discoveries in the south of Romania, where late architecture in the ancient style continued in military and religious life until the end of the sixth century, even if this still has to be confirmed by further research, enable us to establish direct connections between the end of antiquity and the beginning of the Middle Ages. These connections apply to the superior forms of civilization as well as to popular culture.

Returning now to the research at Cuhea in Maramureş, it may be pointed out that the discoveries there are not the only ones in that zone. At Giuleşti, in the Mara valley, where the oldest chancellory documents attest the presence of Dragos's Romanian feudal family at the beginning of the fourteenth century, archaeological excavations show the rubble foundations of the family's Court chapel, built in the Roman style in the thirteenth century. In a neighbouring valley at Onceşti, researchers have identified and searched the ruins of another Romanian feudal family who were refugees, and at Sărăsău, on the Tisa borders, they have found the vestiges of a village which had occupied the same site from the eighth century to the end of the thirteenth, being then recorded in written documents, beginning with the fourteenth century, as a Romanian village. At Sărăsău the traces of a fortress made of earth and wood were also found and the objects discovered there — ceramics, tools, weapons, jewellery — reflect in a convincing way the evolution during several centuries of the old Romanian civilization and also the period of the contact of Daco-Roman culture with the Slav communities up to the late medieval phase.

Research has also revealed, by comparing archaeological discoveries with written sources, the existence of a stratification of ranks, or hierarchy, within the Romanian feudal system in the epoch preceding the foundation of the Romanian medieval states. The "prestatal" feudal organization was composed of *Knezi* who owned several villages (a term derived probably from the German *König, king*), taken over by the Romanians through the channel of the Slavs, and *Jupâni* (a term of Avar origin, meaning big chief) who subordinated *Knezi* of a given region. From among these *Jupâni* there were chosen the *voivodes*, who were higher military and political rulers, at the beginning only periodically and later, when the dignity became hereditary, only symbolically. The contention, promoted in the last century by circles hostile to the national aspirations of the Romanians, that the Romanians did not have a history and an evolution as a people over a long period, that they settled late and were organized as a result of initiatives taken outside Romanian society, has, in the light of archaeological discoveries described here, proved completely unfounded.

In another Romanian "country" in Transylvania, Haţeg, researches in the last two decades have brought to light even more convincing discoveries. Among these are the results of the archaeological investigations of Streisîngeorgiu, not far from the southern border of the Mureş river, where the preserved church proved to be an old Court chapel built in the first half of the twelfth century on the site of a wooden church of the eleventh century. The Romanian feudal family of Streisîngeorgiu was known only through chancellory documents at the end of the fourteenth century, but the inscriptions discovered inside the monument are almost a century earlier, while the jewellery and coins found in the graves round the church go back a further three centuries to a date from which one can follow the history of this complex.

In the mountain area of Bihor to which, according to narrative sources, the *voivode* Menumorut should have retired before the Hungarian attacks, researchers have discovered feudal complexes of the eleventh to thirteenth centuries consisting of residences of the nobility, Court chapels and modest monasteries with wooden fortifications which were also placed around churches built of rubble or around village settlements formed of tens of wooden and earth dwellings. Researches were also carried out at Voivozi in the north of Bihor, at Sînnicolau

Mare, where important archaeological discoveries have been made, including a hoard of gold coins known as Attila's Treasure, at Beiuş, on the borders of the Black Criş river, and at Seghiste in Beiuş county, including the two sites in the central part of Beiuş as well as those of Hălmagiu on the White Criş river valley in the south of the region. At the same time, researches in Banat at Hidia (Caraş-Severin district) and in the Iron Gates region on the northern part of the Danube, occasioned by the construction of the big hydroelectric complex and by the inundation of zones which had dense medieval settlements, enriched considerably the archaeological collection of the south-west of Romania relating to the history of Romania in the tenth to thirteenth centuries.

In the south of the Carpathians, on the territory of Oltenia and Wallachia, two large historical provinces from which the Romanian Country state (Wallachia) was born about 1330, written sources attest a process of political concentration from the first half of the thirteenth century, with the lessening of the military pressure put on the countryside by the Cumans. This information is contained especially in a diploma given by Béla IV, King of Hungary, in 1247 to the Crusader knights of the Order of St John who intended to settle down in this area. The diploma has been preserved, although the arrival of the knights is not confirmed by other documents. In his *History of the Roumanians,* R. W. Seton-Watson points out that Hungarian aggression received a severe check in 1241 when the great Tartar invasion of Genghis Khan, after displacing and crushing the nomad tribes on the Dniester and the Prut, flooded over the Carpathians and for nearly a year wrought havoc in the Apostolic kingdom. Béla IV was crushingly defeated and took refuge in Dalmatia, till the tide slowly flowed back into Asia. Not the least direct effect of this disaster was to remove pressure from the Romanians, and to leave them free to develop on their own lines. "For a generation to come Hungary was occupied in repairing the damage wrought by the Tartar hordes, whose thoroughness is well illustrated by the fact that virtually no documents have survived to us from an earlier period, the royal chancellory having apparently been destroyed and the local administration having for the most part shared its fate. It is this which makes it at once so easy to evolve, and so impossible to prove, rival theories of autochthony and immigration."

In the first half of the thirteenth century there was a Romanian voivodate west of the Olt river under the authority of *Voivode* Litovoi, formed of several large principalities. The centre of this voivodate has not yet been identified by research, but from the diploma quoted above we know that south-west of Transylvania belonged to it, probably as a result of a "settling-down" of the type evoked in the diploma. At the same time there was another Romanian voivodate east of the Olt river under the authority of *Voivode* Seneslau, whose residence has been identified as being at Curtea de Argeş. In this town, capital of the Romanian country by the middle of the fourteenth century, researchers have found under monuments of 1330-70 the foundations of constructions of the thirteenth century and even of the end of the twelfth. These are linked to the voivodate of Argeş mentioned in the documents and prove that the political unification of the territories south of the Carpathians was made in favour of the princely dynasty of Curtea de A⌐geş, which existed there from the twelfth century and which assumed by 1300 the dignity of Great *Voivode* or *Domn* (from the Latin *dominus),* which means prince, of the entire Romanian Country.

The political centre of Curtea de Argeş does not represent the only capital of a "country" known in the thirteenth century south of the Carpathians. At Cetăţeni in Dîmboviţa valley at the foot of the mountains researchers have recently discovered and investigated the remains of another Romanian feudal centre of the twelfth and thirteenth centuries which consisted of a fortress, several churches and traces of settlements situated in sheltered places. It has been established that a *voivode* lived at Cetăţeni. His name is at present unknown but some historians identify him with the legendary "Negru Voda" who came from Transylvania to the north of Wallachia and ruled simultaneously parts of south Transylvania in Făgăraş Country. Thus they have created a very interesting political image of Romanian political formations which included territories on both parts of the Carpathians, in Oltenia, in Wallachia and probably also in Moldavia, because the mountains did not represent frontiers for the original inhabitants. On the contrary, they represented the supporting column of a society which sought the means of conservation of its historical being and its own political expression.

Romanian territorial structures of the pre-feudal "country" type are also attested by written sources as being east of the Carpathians on the territory of the future Moldavia. They appear under the term "peasant republics" in Vrancea Country in the south of Moldavia in the town of Cîmpulung which covers in the north the main course of the Moldova river and east, towards the Dniester, the so-called Tigheciu forest. Documentary sources do not contain enough material to allow us to speculate about these territorial structures until the fourteenth century, in the middle of which the medieval state of Moldavia was created by the military and "settling-down" of those who came from Maramureş and those who were in the battle against the Mongols of the Golden Horde. But the recently published account of archaeological discoveries in the Somuzul Mare basin, the vestiges found in the excavations at Suceava, capital of Moldavia in the fourteenth to sixteenth centuries, and the recent spectacular discoveries in the centre of the town of Jassy, another former capital of Moldavia, when large urban works were built, allow us to resume the survey of the chronological order of events in the eleventh and twelfth centuries. One cannot speak about the exodus of the Romanian population from one side of the Carpathians to the other (as has been done to support the idea, advanced by political interests of the modern era) as a major shift in population. The "settling-down" was only the movement of small military and political groups in a territory which had been inhabited in a unitary way by the same Romanian population from early times. At Rădăuţi, which in the fourteenth century was, for a short time, the capital of Moldavia and in which an episcopal seat was founded, researchers have pointed out that the grafting of the newcomers from Maramureş, was in a Romanian centre of feudal authority which existed a few generations earlier than the time of the "settling-down". The grave of Bogdan I, the *voivode* who came from Maramureş, discovered in the old church at Rădăuţi, with a rich and significant funeral inventory, increased the number of older voivodal graves at that place.

By the end of the thirteenth and the beginning of the fourteenth centuries (though for Moldavia only by the middle of the fourteenth century), the three Romanian medieval states had asserted themselves on the European political scene. As a dependent voivodate of the Hungarian kingdom, Transylvania enjoyed for a short time an independent position during the domination of the *voivodes* of the Borsa and Kan dynasties. With the setting up of the new Angevin dynasty on the throne of Hungary, the independent tendencies of the Transylvanian voivodate, based on the age of its own institutions and on Romanian demographic features, were hindered and could only be manifested occasionally during a period of social and political crisis, but their orientation was towards the other Romanian historical provinces. An example was provided in 1600 when the first political unification of the three Romanian medieval principalities took place under Michael the Brave, but this did not last long. However, this unification was a foretaste of the great union of all the territories inhabited by Romanians after the end of the First World War.

The tendencies of the Hungarian Crown during the thirteenth century to overstep to the south and to the east the boundaries of the Carpathians helped to decide the affirmation of the independent status of the Romanian Country (Wallachia) and Moldavia in the fight with the Hungarian forces and with the Mongols (Tartars). A first attempt to remove the Hungarian suzerainty, made in 1274-5 by the *voivode* of Oltenia, failed. A similar attemps was made again after 1320 by *voivode* Basarab from Curtea de Argeş. In a confrontation in 1330 with the army of the Hungarian King Carol Robert of the Angevin dynasty, the army of the Romanian Country gained at Posada a victory which was the equivalent, from a military and political point of view, of a birth certificate of the Romanian principality south of the Carpathians as an independent medieval state.

Two decades later Bogdan I, former *voivode* of Maramureş, succeeded east of the Carpathians in a similar action against the army sent by Louis I, successor to Carol Robert on the throne of Hungary, with the result that in the following years the boundaries of Moldavia stretched from the sea to the Dniester, including the territories inhabited by the Romanians and dominated by the Tartars of the Golden Horde.

The geographical peculiarities of the Romanian territories, as well as circumstances of the political history of the Carpathian-Danubian-Pontic area at the end of the first millennium, determined the organization of Romanian state life in medieval patterns in all three separate principalities. But the antecedents of this moment of political history attest an impressive unity in the evolution of the regions inhabited by the descendants of eastern Romanity, a unity apparent in the aspects of material and spiritual culture, as well as in the organization of society in the successive periods of the formation of the Romanian people.

The basic Thracian-Geto-Dacian element of the population in the whole territory passed through a process of Romanization which lasted for a few centuries, resulting in the formation of the Daco-Roman society present in the fourth to sixth centuries AD from the territory of the northern Carpathians to the Balkan mountains. For a long period the mixture of Dacians lived in the "shadow" of the short-lived kingdoms founded by the Germanic, Turanian and Slav migratory races, but they maintained their identity and traditions by a modest life organized in the frame of the village community. The slow progress in the evolution of the race realized in the second half of the first millenium AD led to the completion of the formative process of the Romanian people in the ninth and tenth centuries when similar processes of political history took place in the majority of the other regions of the Continent. Moreover, one can establish parallels between the periods and forms registered by the Romanians in the process of their ethnic formation and of the foundation of their medieval states and those registered by the other neo-Latin peoples of Europe.

Some Considerations

Now that we have reached a certain stage in our historical and archaeological survey, let us pause and look back on the ground covered to date.

Many readers will be surprised by the thoroughness of the surveys carried out by Romanian archaeologists and historians but the reason for this is what they see as the need to establish a national identity in so troubled an area as the Balkans, where territorial disputes involving minorities abound. An article on the Balkans in an issue of *The Economist* of 20 April 1985 ended with the conclusion that, "History lies heavily on the Balkans. In one sense, the bitter east-west division of Europe seems less unnatural here than in other regions, because the local traditions of hostility are so much stronger than those of neighbourliness. It would be unwise to assume the stability of the pattern of ideological and strategic alignment that has been imposed on the region since 1945. The Balkans are still the Balkans.".

What has particularly concerned the Romanians is that their claim that they are descendants, in the main, of Romans intermarried with Dacians has been disputed for reasons advanced by a German geographer and espoused by Hungarians who still claim Transylvania as a Hungarian land lost by them because they were on the losing side in the 1914-18 war. For this claim to succeed, it has to be proved that Transylvania was largely an empty land when the Hungarian tribes arrived there in AD 896. It is claimed in the entry on Transylvania in *Chambers's Encyclopaedia* that Romanians figured only in one area, and there only for a short period, but archaeological research, the only one that can carry conviction in the absence of documents destroyed during the invasions of the Mongols, proves that this was not so and that the Romanians had been established for centuries over wide areas of Transylvania. The significance of the archaeological finds has been partly obscured by the continuing clamour of Hungarian propaganda about the alleged ill treatment of the large Hungarian minority in Transylvania. I have interviewed representatives, civil and religious, of the Hungarians in Transylvania and have found that they do not subscribe to this campaign fuelled from outside the country. It is important that we should not allow ourselves to be distracted by this campaign but should concentrate on the significance of the archaeological discoveries which are too little known because the literature about them is largely in Romanian publications which do not get a wide circulation abroad.

For many scholars, close observers of the Balkan scene, questions still abound. For instance, in a review of a book on Romanian history in *The Times Literary Supplement* of 4 October 1985, the Romanian scholar Virgil Nemoianu, who teaches comparative literature at the Catholic University of America at Washington, DC, said that:

A surprising amount of worthwhile research on the Romanian past (much of it published in the past forty years) is now available, but existing surveys are either too dependent on the details or fret too much over the disputed and blank areas (the "historical enigmas"). Thus the language clearly descends from the eastern branch of Low Vulgate Latin but does this prove anything about the ethnic make-up of the inhabitants ? Probably not, but where else can these be placed in any typology of European nationalities ? Was there a continuity of population in the Dacian province between the withdrawal of the Roman legions and garrisons under the Emperor Aurelian (AD 275) and 1000-1200 when reliable historical information is once again available? Common sense would say yes, but the data are too spotty and contradictory to allow for certainty.

I agree with Nemoianu that common sense suggests that there was a continuity of the population after Aurelian withdrew his legions to south of the Danube (R. W. Seton-Watson takes the same view) but I do not agree with him in believing that the data are "too spotty and contradictory" to allow for certainty. The certainty is provided by the results of archaeological discoveries, particularly of the content of cemeteries as well as that of fortresses and settlements. There is no dispute that following Trajan's victories intermarriage took place between Dacians and Romans and that it should be expected that excavations of settlements over the province up to AD 275 should provide proof of the co-existence of both civilizations. Proof of the continuity of the population north of the Danube *after* Aurelian's withdrawal could only come from archaeological discoveries which included objects, ceramics, coins and inscriptions. I have set out the evidence for this in the preceding chapters: it is not, I suggest, "spotty and contradictory", but being so new to Western readers it will be some time before it is assimilated, and it will certainly not be welcomed by those more anxious to continue a controversy about the origins of the population of Transylvania than establish the facts.

But quite apart from the problem posed by Aurelian's withdrawal, to which, thanks to the work of archaeologists and historians, an answer has now been given, other problems remain to be solved, such as the site of old battles for example, Posada, where Basarab I defeated the Hungarian King Carol Robert of Anjou in 1330, and fortresses such as Helis, where Lysimachus, King of Thrace, was taken after his defeat by King Dromichaites, leader of a union of Getian tribes, in 291 BC. There is still a great deal to be learnt about the Dacians, ancestors of the Romanians, and civilizations brought to the coast of the Black Sea by Greeks and Romans. Further excavations of fortresses may bring to light inscriptions on blocks of stone carved there by Greek master masons.

Nothing attracts more public attention in archaeology than finds of treasure, of which there has been a rich harvest in Romania. It is fortunate for the state that the work of archaeologists in Romania is not disturbed by the activities of treasure-hunters armed with metal-detectors, something which is common in Britain. Treasures unearthed in Romania remain there to be admired in museums by the general public, a change from the times of foreign domination when they were dispersed abroad. It is possible that future excavations will bring to light more objects of religious worship, whether household gods similar to the *glykon*, the only sculpture of its kind in the world, in the Constanţa Museum, or aids to devotion in the early days of Christianity. It is most encouraging that excavations are still continuing in the ancient cities of Histria, Constanţa (Tomis) and Callatis (Mangalia) in Dobrudja.

Appendix: The Stones of Sarmizegetusa

Excavations at Sarmizegetusa in 1872 uncovered at this ancient capital of the Dacians sanctuaries used for religious purposes before they were destroyed by the Romans after their victory in AD 106. The researchers found the damaged remains of thirteen sanctuaries, consisting of one very large circle, one small circle and the rest rectangular in shape. What were found were, in the main, circular stones in which columns, arranged in regular patterns, had once stood. The columns had been broken by the victorious Romans before their withdrawal but two small columns still remained in the smaller circular sanctuary; it is believed that in the larger sanctuary the columns were twenty times higher. Some of them were of stone and others of wood. (Part of a well-preserved wooden column is in Deva Museum). Because of the centuries spent under the protecting cover of soil, all the base stones were still in position, in contrast to the situation at Stonehenge in Wiltshire, built eighteen hundred years earlier (in stages between 2800 BC and 1100 BC), where some of the stones are missing, although the position where they once stood may be ascertained from holes.

Stonehenge, it is now generally conceded, was once an observatory, but was Sarmizegetusa also an observatory as well as a place for religious practices? One who believes that it was is Dr Emil Poenaru, Professor of History at Braşov University, where I discussed the matter with him. The principal cults at Sarmizegetusa, he said, were those of the worship of the sun — one stone was found in the form of the sun with rays — and the sacrifice of the brave every five years. Only the best people were sacrificed, as the offering had to be a worthy one: there was no question of criminals being chosen as deserving of death. Other cults involved the observance of the cycle of time and the apprehension of infinity.

Professor Poenaru believes that the first step to a rational understanding of time was its measurement. Man took that step prompted by everyday needs — to set the time for agricultural works, for moving the herds, for hunting game or waiting for the waters to overflow, as in Egypt. But by measuring time, by setting convention- al marks, man also understood that he measured his own life. Similarly, social organizations tended to depict the objective physical flow of time, to which end com- paratively stable reference marks were required. How could such reference marks be set?

The heavenly bodies in the sky with their observable sequence and minute repeatability of movement seem to rotate above the Earth as if to mark time. The sun, the source of light, which nearly all the people worshipped at the beginning, marks the first time-measuring unit — the interval between two successive appearances, the twenty-four-hour day, a unit also conditioning human activity by its alternation of light and darkness. Another body, the moon, with its regular nocturnal appearance, changes its aspect in a regular sequence, which makes it possible to foretell the number of days between two identical aspects (lunations) and thus was a reference point for a higher time unit, the month. The time required by the sun to get back to the same position in its observable movement becomes the time unit called the solar year. By observing the sky, man could see that sun is preceded at sunrise or followed at sunset by con- stantly different trains of stars, the sequence of which observed a certain regular pattern, and that in our hemi- sphere the sky and the stars in it are slowly moving round the fixed north star.

On the basis of these observations calendars were devised, dividing time into units to which distinctive meanings were attached (working days, holidays). In that way, social time developed as a concept. Professor Poenaru said that, when they considered the sanctuaries at Sarmizegetusa, observers had the impression that their component parts, by their arrangement, number, orien- tation and size, enclosed certain meanings undeciphered as yet. But, taking the premise that they comprised a calendar as a basis, they also had to admit that the information these monuments contained is coded and richer in significance, if more difficult to "read", than word writing. The Geto-Dacians, incidentally, did not know how to write; the Greek amphorae they imitated bore a seal but no letters. Neither is there any writing on their coins, which were imitations of Macedonian models.

After a topometric survey made with the help of Dr Kiss Arpad, Assistant Professor at Braşov University, Dr Poenaru, with his colleagues C. Samoilă and S. Bobancu, undertook to "decode" the monuments by analysing them as calendars and as evidence of astronomic geometric and trigonometric knowledge.

The smaller circular sanctuary consists of 114 elements, of which 13 were slabs separating 13 groups of posts arranged as follows: 8 groups×8 posts each, 1 group×7 posts, 3 groups×8 posts, 1 group×6 posts (101 posts plus 13 slabs in all).

The larger circular sanctuary consists of three concentric circles and an apsidal building in the middle with a symmetrical axis and a threshold axis.

The outer circle was made of 104 andesite abutting blocks.

The next circle consisted of 210 elements, of which 30 were slabs separating 30 groups with 6 posts each.

The third circle consisted of 4 groups of slabs separating 4 groups of posts according to the following pattern from the threshold axis and threshold, 4 counter clockwise: 17 posts-4 slabs-18 posts-3 slabs-16 posts-4 slabs-17 posts-3 slabs (68 posts plus 14 slabs in all).

The central apse consisted of 2 groups of slabs separating 2 groups of posts taken from the threshold axis and threshold, 3 counter clockwise: 13 posts-2 slabs-21 posts-2 slabs (34 posts plus 4 slabs in all).

Professor Poenaru's team tested a large number of original algorithms to develop a unitary system of interpretation different from those suggested by other authors. They considered that, with the least natural time division, easily perceivable and biologically felt — the twenty-four hour day — any calendar should mark the flow of time by quantifying it into days. With this idea in mind, they considered the following equivalence for the smaller circular sanctuary: 1 andesite post equalled 1 day and night and 1 slab equalled 1 separation mark. In that way the circumference of the smaller circular sanctuary equalled 101 days.

Dr Poenaru pointed out that :

We can see that by covering three or four times the circumference $(101 \times 3 = 303; 101 \times 4 = 404)$ values widely different from that of an astronomic year (365) are obtained. Therefore, a circumference multiplier M should be sought to yield a value closest to an integer standing for an integral number of years (R). Computations have shown that $R = 13$ and $M = 47$ (when the calendar lag is minimal), that is 13 astronomic years equals 47 times the circumference of the smaller sanctury — a case in which only a one day (maybe holiday) correction was required. We have thus come to the first major conclusion: the Dacian calendar covered a 13-year span of time with one correction day. The same calendar shows that there were 47 weeks in a Dacian year. Therefore, the division of the smaller sanctuary into 13 groups is no accident; on the contrary, it is purposeful and has the advantage that it explains why the Dacian years always begin with the first day in a group, hence always ending with the last day of a group, and all the 13 first days in the 13 groups were only once first days of the year during one cycle. That the Dacian years did not begin or end with any one of the days of the week (the equivalence 1 group = 1 week is suggested) is a remarkable quality that not even the present-day calendar has.

Dr Poenaru and his colleagues maintained that the circle of the greater 104-slab circular sanctuary allowed for the Dacian century to be recorded globally, but because of the uniformity of the slabs it did not distinguish between the thirteen-year cycles or between the fifty-two-year periods evidenced by the central apsidal building. "By ascribing a one-year value to one andesite drum, we have come to the highly important conclusion that there was a system to record every year in a thirteen-year cycle, the 52 $(4 \times 13 = 52)$ year Dacian period, in the same way as the Dacian century, by going twice over the quadrangle perimeter. In consideration of the numerical composition of the outer circle of the larger circular sanctuary, conjugated to the 4×13 rectangular sanctuary, it seems that the number of years of a Dacian century (104) turns from supposition into certainty."

Summing up, Dr Poenaru said that the sanctuaries at Sarmizegetusa were made of stone slabs, stone and wooden posts and stone drums which, in the archaeologists' opinion, were column stands. The use of slabs as "marks" went back to prehistoric times. The Roman physician Galen in his *De Simplis* spoke of the mysterious and incantatory "Thracian border stones" symbolizing more than mere border marks.

In the architecture of the sanctuary the slabs were intended to separate the groups of days, weeks or years, preserving the separatory function of the "Thracian stones". Even when there were 104 slabs arranged in a circular pattern, symbolizing the 104 years of the Dacian century, they followed the circular outline bordering the larger circular sanctuary, hence implying a separatory function too.

The four slabs in the central apse of the larger circular sanctuary marking the correction days every thirteen-year cycle were also used to separate these cycles. These slabs (two thresholds taken at a time) also separated the trimesters of the year, their functions overlapping.

The posts, as architectural elements of the calendar, when of stone stood for the days and when taller, made of wood, marked the correction days or they served to record the weeks.

The columns or, by extrapolation, the drums, which in the calendar architecture were symbols (and marks) of the higher time units in general (years, the thirteen-year cycle etc), were also ancient "signs" full of significance.

The posts in the inner circle and the apse in the larger circular sanctuary were altogether different from the day posts — that is, they were tall, four-edged posts made of wood fixed with spikes (between nine to thirteen each, as the archaeologists have found), ending in hooks to which "marks" were attached, serving several purposes, as evidence of the correction days, the number of weeks in a year and so on.

In the system of significance of the sanctuary elements, the drums acquired the value of higher time units. One drum equalled one year or one thirteen-year-cycle. The equivalence with the different higher time units was also suggested by different sizes. Thus the drums of the 4×13 sanctuary (equivalent to one year each) were of smaller size than those of the 4×10 sanctuary, each symbolizing a thirteen-year cycle.

These elements carrying equivalent meanings as referred to the time-measuring units were involved in the calendar mechanism by simple addition, a principle observed also in the corrections since the Dacian calendars (for civil and religious purposes) were so conceived as to lag generally behind the exact astronomic time, requiring correction by addition to enhance the accuracy. No matter the magnitude of the corrected time unit, the correction unit added was always the sameone day.

The principle of the measured time lagging behind the exact astronomic time observed a basic reality viz. that it was time flowing, the time going by which was being measured, not future time, hence unlived time, for the measurement preceding the flow of time was theoretical and artificial in character. Therefore, starting from the hypothesis of the common origin of astronomic time and of time as reflected in the calendar measurement, the lag of the latter allowed for the new origins to draw nearer by adding a cell unit (one day).

The wise "architects" of the sanctuaries undertook the "reform" of the 104-century system not only to improve the accuracy of the calendar but also because in the 104-year century system the one-day correction used every 520 years (the "millennium") made calendar time outdistance astronomic time by about 1.5 hours — hence the inference that the mean calendar time was ahead of astronomic time for roughly one year. This "error" of getting ahead of astronomic time by marking the one-day correction is shared by our present calendar, Dr Poenaru said, "but if we, the people of twentieth-century civilization, have not found yet a way to reform our calendar and discard the error, all the more praiseworthy are our forefathers who reformed their calendar — shifting to the ninety-one-year century — which not only did not get ahead of exact astronomic time the moment the one-day correction was made but resulted in such precision that we can say that the moment the correction was made, every 2,275 years, the origin of calendar time and that of the exact astronomic time almost overlapped."

Dr Poenaru considered that, such being the situation, we could say that none of the calendars ever devised by man conceived of a reform which left unaltered the mechanism of the calendar proper while ensuring utmost accuracy solely by changing the number of years in a century. Of all the performances of the calendars at Sarmizegetusa, possibly the most amazing was that of the fluctuating years within a thirteen-year cycle.

All the calendars in the world had to solve the same question — they had to use integers, i.e. days, to measure a fractional magnitude, the year, which has not a fluctuating number of days (365.242198 days as we know today). One of the most interesting solutions was that anticipated by an old Brahmanic calendar taken over by the Romans under Caesar through the astronomer Sosigenes of Alexandria, using a four-year cycle in which three were 365-day years and the fourth was a 366-day year (with a 365.25 day mean year). With its subsequent corrections, this cycle has been preserved to this day.

The cycle in the Dacian calendar had a wider range of years — thirteen — with fluctuations ranging from 364 to 367 days. The fluctuating day values of the years within the thirteen-year cycle were expressed in the construction pattern of the smaller circular sanctuary to the effect that two of the day groups were not eight-day groups as the other eleven were but seven- and six-day groups respectively. "By the functional and simple mathematical solutions it incorporates (and expressed geometrically) the smaller circular sanctuary is the finest 'work of art' that human thought has devised in its endeavour to quantify time."

Professor Poenaru's explanation of the Dacian calendar may, at first, be thought unnecessarily complex, but on second thoughts it will be seen to be a masterly interpretation of the significance of stones buried for many centuries. The meaning of the stones, it seems to me, could only be interpreted by the way they were arranged, for no written interpretation was possible ; the Dacians did not have a writter language. Dr Poenaru considers that Sarmizegetusa and Stonehenge share the distinction of being the only sanctuaries whose meaning is clear; those in central America and China are not as clear.

Because of the remoteness of Sarmizegetusa, now known as Grădiștea Muncelului, it has been difficult of access to the general public, but roads to the spot are now being rebuilt and should be finished by the end of 1986. However, plans have been made for reproductions of the stones and columns to be placed on the site and the originals to be sent to museums and laboratories. Sarmizegetusa may lack the grandeur of Stonehenge but it retains the same air of mystery which is attached to the rites of an ancient race, rites imperfectly understood today.

The major Geto-Dacian centres *(davae)* in the last three centuries prior to the Roman conquest were also religious centres. Though the information we have is rather scarce, the few discoveries that have been made are satisfactory as providing evidence for this assertion for some of the centres. Significant in this respect are the sanctuaries at Pecica (circular) and Barboşi (rectangular) and the apsidal buildings at Popeşti, Cetăţeni, Cîrlomăneşti and Pecica considered to have a religious character, alongside the traces of the places of worship with underground cells at Ocniţa in Oltenia. We may add to these a number of fire pits with offerings (Sprîncenata), decorated fire pits that served for worship (Popeşti, Cîrlomăneşti), zoo- and anthropomorphic religious statuettes (Ocniţa, Crăsani, Cîrlomăneşti, Gruiu-Darii, Pietroasele, Poiana etc) and ritual pits rather frequently unearthed. There are some *davae* where religious-worship finds are grouped together so it may be assumed that they make up true "sacred zones".

But to return to Sarmizegetusa, excavations at Bîtca Doamnei, known as "Moldavia's Sinaia" (Sinaia is a favourite mountain resort within easy reach of Bucharest) have revealed traces of two sanctuaries whose plan and stone-drum rows are analogous to those of the Dacian sanctuaries identified in the Orăştie Mountains. One of the sanctuaries, partially overlying the southern tower, is dated to a stage earlier than the fortification. The other one — outside the surrounding wall but within a short distance on a terrace purposefully arranged — belongs to the second phase of the stronghold, in all probability. The north-south orientation of the row of drums in the first sanctuary, and the west-east one of the latter, is a faithful image of the orientation of the drums at Sarmizegetusa.

Who were the designers of the sanctuary at Sarmizegetusa? Almost certainly the priests, among whom could have been Deceneu, high priest and adviser to King Burebista. Taking as a basis the texts of Dion Chrysostomos, who had lived in Dacia for several years, Jordanes (fifth century), describing the activities of Deceneu, said that, "On explaining the theory of the twelve signs of the zodiac, he showed them [the Dacians] the movement of the planets and all astronomic secrets, how the moon was waxing and waning, and how the fiery globe of the sun outsized the earth; he told them the names and the signs under which the 346 stars pass on their fast way from sunrise to sunset to get closer or farther away from the celestial pole."

Further research will almost certainly throw fresh light on the Dacians and their remarkable theories of time.

Bibliography

In this Bibliography I have mentioned some of the more recent books on archaeology and history but have not included, with one or two exceptions, references to articles in periodicals of a specialist nature. Those who wish to consult them should turn to the Bibliography in Ligia Bârzu's book on Romanian continuity which I have quoted. In *Pages of History*, nos 3-4, 1981, this author adds a further Bibliography to her review of André du Nay's book *The early history of the Romanian language* (Illinois, 1977) which she analyses in the light of archaeological evidence.

Alexandrescu, P., *Histria, IV* (Bucharest, 1978).

Armbruster, A., *Assimilation et résistance à la culture Gréco-Romaine dans le monde ancien* (Bucharest—Paris, 1976).

Barnea, I., *Arta creştină în România* (Bucharest, 1981).

Barnea, I., and others *Tropaeum Traiani 1, Cetatea (Tropaeum Traiani I, Fortress)* (Bucharest, 1979).

Bârzu, Ligia, *Continuitatea Creaţiei Materiale şi Spirituale a Poporului Român pe Teritoriul fostei Dacii* (Bucharest, 1979). The English edition of this work, translated by Christina Krikorian and published in the same year in Bucharest, is *Continuity of the Romanian People's Material and Spiritual Production in the Territory of Former Dacia.*

Berciu, D., *Buridava Dacică* (Bucharest, 1981).

Bichir, Gh., *Cultura Carpică* (Bucharest, 1973). English edition : *Archaeology and History of the Carpi*, Parts 1-11, BAR supplementary series 16 (11) (London, 1976).

Bichir, Gh., *Geto-Dacii din Muntenia în Epoca Romană* (Bucharest, 1984).

Comşa, M., *Cultura Materială Veche Românească* (Bucharest, 1978).

Crişan, I. H., *Ceramica Daco-Getică* (Bucharest, 1969).

Crişan, I. H., *Burebista şi Epoca Sa* (Bucharest, 1977).

Daicoviciu, H., *Dacia de la Burebista la Cucerirea Romană* (Cluj, 1972).

Diaconu, Petre, *Păcuiul lui Soare. Cetatea Bizantină* (Bucharest, 1972).

Diaconu, Petre, and Baraschi, Silvia, *Păcuiul lui Soare 11. Aşezăre Medievală (Păcuiul lui Soare, 11. A medieval Settlement* (Bucharest, 1977).

Diaconu, Petre, *Les Coumans au Bas-Danube aux XI et XII Siècles* (Bucharest, 1978).

Dolinescu-Ferche, S., *Aşezări din Secolele III şi VI e.n. în sud-vestul Munteniei* (Bucharest, 1974).

Florescu, Gr., and Petolescu C. C., *Inscripţiile Daciei Romane, 11 (Inscriptions of Roman Dacia, 11)* (Bucharest, 1977).

Glodariu, I., Costea, Fl., Ciupea, I. *Comana de Jos. Aşesările de Epocă Dacică Şi Prefeudală* (Braşov and Făgăraş, 1980).

Gostar, N., *Cetăţi Dacice din Moldova* (Bucharest, 1969).

Horedt, K., *Contribuţii La Istoria Transilvaniei în Sec. IV-XIII* (Bucharest, 1958).

Ioniţă, I., *Din Istoria şi Civilizaţia Dacilor Liberi* (Iaşi, 1982).

Iorga, N., *Histoire des Roumains*, Vol. I, II. *Le Sceau de Rome* (Bucharest, 1937).

Mitrea, B., şi Preda, C., *Necropole din sec. IV e.n. în Muntenia* (Bucharest, 1966).

Oţetea, A., and MacKenzie, A., *A Concise History of Romania* (London, 1985).

Pârvan, V., *Getica* (Bucharest, 1926).

Pârvan, V., *Dacia* (Bucharest, 1967).

Pârvan, V., *Începuturile Vieţii Romane la Gurile Dunării* (Bucharest, 1974).

Pascu, Ş., *A History of Transylvania*, translated by D. R. Ladd (Detroit, 1983).

Paul, I., *Praehistorische Zeitschrift* (Berlin, 1981). There is a useful section on ceramics, with illustrations.

Popa, R., *Ţara Maramureşului în Veacul al XIV-lea* (Bucharest, 1970).

Popa, R., *Aux Débuts de l'Histoire Médiévale Roumaine. Problèmes Spécifiques et Résultats des Recherches Récents in Anuario de Estudio Mediévales*, 13 (Barcelona, 1983).

Popescu, E., *Inscripţiile Greceşti şi Latine din Secolele IV-XIII Descoperite în România* (the 4th-13th Greek and Latin inscriptions discovered in Romania (Bucharest, 1976).

Popilian, Gh., *Necropola Daco-Romană de la Locusteni* (Craiova, 1980).

Pippidi, D. M., *Scythica Minora. Recherches sur les Colonies Grecques du Littoral Roumain de la Mer Noire* (Bucharest, 1975).

Pippidi, D. M., (ed.). *Relations between the Autochthonous Population and the Migratory Populations on the Territory of Romania* (Bucharest, 1975).

Pippidi, D. M., and Popescu, E., *Epigraphica* (Bucharest, 1977).

Preda, C., *Callatis. Necropole Romano-Bizantină* (Bucharest, 1980).

Preda, C., *Mondele Geto-Dacilo* (Bucharest, 1973).

Protase, D., *Problema Continuităţii în Lumina Arheologiei şi Numismaticii* (Bucharest, 1966).

Protase, D., *Riturile Funerare la Daci, şi Daco-Romani* (Bucharest, 1971).

Protase, D., *Un Cimitir Dacic din Epoca Romană în Soporul de Cîmpie* (A Dacian cemetery from Roman times at Soporul de Cîmpie) (Bucharest, 1976).

Russu, I. I., *Inscripţiile Daciei Romane, III* (Inscriptions of Roman Dacia, III). (Bucharest, 1977). He is also the author of an earlier book on inscriptions.

Russu, I. I., *Elemente Traco-Getice în Imperiul Roman şi Byzantin* (Thraco-Getic elements in the Roman Empire and Byzantium) (Bucharest, 1976).

Russu, I. I., *Etnogeneza Românilor* (Bucharest, 1981).

Seton-Watson, R. W., *History of the Roumanians* (Cambridge, 1934).

Suceveanu, Al., *Viaţa Economică în Dobrogea Romană. Secolele I-III e.n.* (Economic life in Roman Dobrudja. The First and Second Centuries AD), (Bucharest, 1977).

Tudor, D., *Teritoriul Est-Carpatic în Veacurile V-XI* (Iaşi, 1984).

Tudor, D., *Civilizaţia Romanică la Est de Carpaţi în Sec. V—VIII* (Iaşi, 1984).

Tudor, D., *Oltenia Romană* (Roman Oltenia), (Bucharest, 1978).

Vulpe, R., *Studia Thracologica* (Bucharest, 1980).

Zaharia, E., *Săpăturile de la Dridu* (Bucharest, 1967).

Zaharia, E., *Populaţia Românească în Transilvania în Secolele VII-VIII. Cimitirul nr. 2 de la Bratei* (The Romanian Population in the 7th-8th centuries in Transylvania. Cemetery no. 2 at Bratei) (Bucharest, 1977).

List of Illustrations

Fourth century AD donarium discovered at Biertan, Transylvania

Items from an inventory of discoveries at Pietroasa, Velt and Chiojd

A gold medallion with the bust of Aphrodite found at Callatis (Mangalia)

Marble statue of Priapis, third or fourth century, Callatis

Miniature gilt ceramic of a Greek fighter, fourth century BC

Fifth century gold and silver vessels from Cauzeşti, Pietroasa and Apahida

Famous fifth century treasures from Pietroasa

Ruins of a pier at Păcuiul lui Soare island Constanţa county, end of tenth century AD

Chapel of a feudal family from Densus, Hunedoara county, with traces of construction from the thirteenth century

Chapel of a feudal family from Streisîngiorgiu, Hunedoara county

Ruins of a chapel belonging to a feudal family from Giuleşti, Maramureş county, thirteenth century AD

Tower of a house of a feudal family named Densus, thirteenth to fourteenth century AD

The museum at Adamclisi with original panels (metopes) from monument erected by Emperor Trajan to celebrate his triumph

Part of the archaeological park at Constanţa

Map of Romania   pp. 22-3

Index

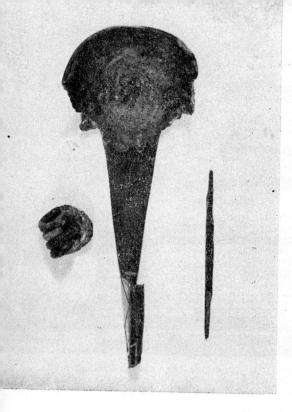

A Dacian *fibula* (clasp or brooch) of the spoon type shown on a tomb- stone at Brukenthal Museum. Discovered at Tilişca, Sibiu county, *c.* 100 BC—AD 100

Skeleton of a Dacian in a circular grave

The reconstructed monument at Adamclisi, Dobrudja, erected by Emperor Trajan in AD 106—9 to celebrate his victory over the Dacians and other allies of Decebalus, the Dacian king, in AD 102.

One of the rectangular sanctuaries at Sarmizegetusa, the fortress headquarters of the Dacian kings

Aerial view of Dacian settlement of the first century BC—AD first century in the Olt Valley. The settlement is in the middle of the picture

Geto-Dacian silver vessels from the first century BC, part of the
treasure from Sîncrăieni, Transylvania

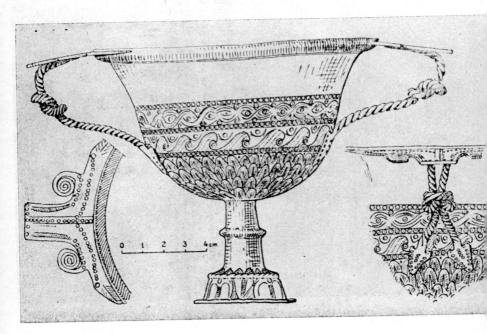

Geto-Dacian clay vessels, first century BC

Geto-Dacian gold and silver helmets and vessels, first century BC

Female figure on a tombstone,
Tomi, third century

Funeral medallion on tombstone,
c. AD 100—300 discovered at
Apoldul de Sus, Sibiu county and
now at Brukenthal Museum. The
husband is Roman, the wife Dacian as shown by the clasp on
her dress

Fragment of a second or third century sarcophagus with fanciful scenes,
Museum of Archaeology, Constanţa

A Roman grave of the second or third century AD. Household objects
including pottery were buried with the ashes

A *donarium* (votive offering) of the fourth century AD discovered at
Biertan, Transylvania

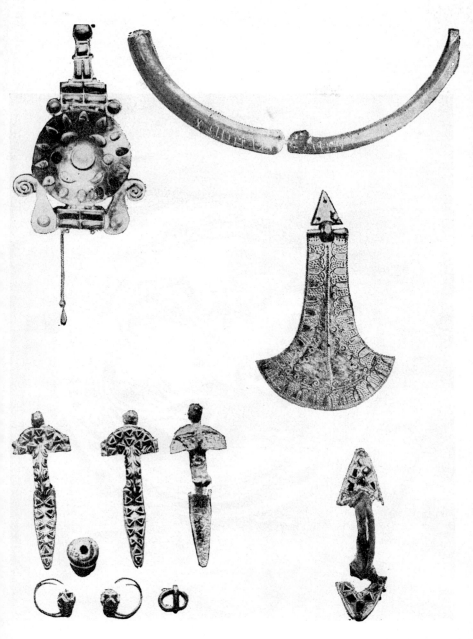

Items from an inventory of discoveries at Pietroasa, Velt and Chiojd, fifth century AD

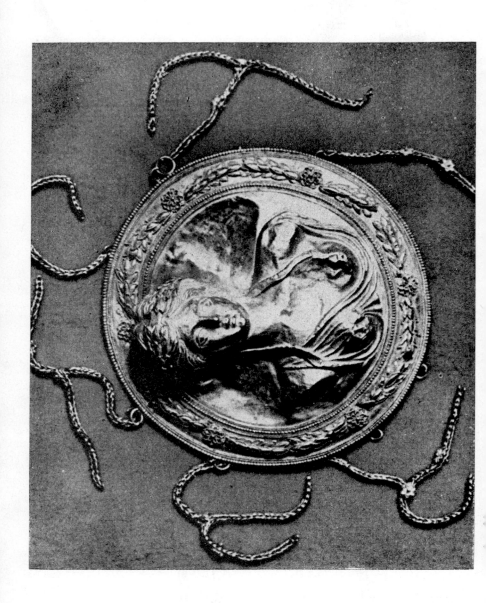

Miniature gilt ceramic of a
Greek fighter, fourth century
BC, Callatis

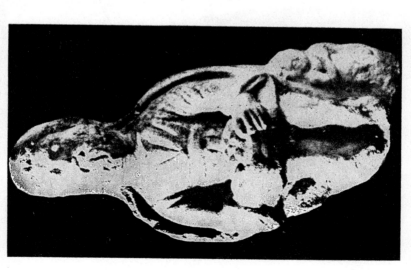

Marble statue of Priapis, third or
fourth century, Callatis

Fifth century gold and silver vessels from Cauzești, Pietroasa and Apahida

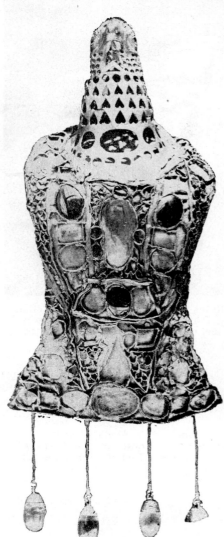

Famous fifth century treasures from
Pietroasa. Above, a gold necklace-
Right : "The Golden Hen", one of
the most important finds. Below : a
gold basket

Ruins of a pier of a Byzantine citadel at Păcuiul lui Soare island, Saliţy village, county of Constanţa, end of tenth century AD

Chapel of a feudal family from Densus county of Hunedoara. A Roman monument, later used as a church, with traces of construction from the thirteenth century

Chapel of a feudal family from Streisingiorgiu, county of Hunedoara. Monument built in the first half of the twelfth century with material from a Roman ruin on a site once occupied by a wooden church

Ruins of a chapel belonging to a feudal family from Giuleşti, county of Maramureş, thirteenth century AD

Tower of a house of a feudal family named Densus, thirteenth-to-fourteenth century AD

The museum at Adamclisi houses the original panels (*metopes*) showing scenes from Emperor Trajan's battle with the Dacians, AD 102

Part of the archaeological park at Constanţa